MW01041968

ASSARACUS

A JOURNAL OF GAY POETRY

ISSUE 15

SIBLING RIVALRY PRESS
LITTLE ROCK, ARKANSAS
siblingrivalrypress.com

PUBLISHERS & EDITORS

Bryan Borland & Seth Pennington

Cover art, *Slash*, by Seth Ruggles Hiler. Used by permission.

Sibling Rivalry Press
PO Box 26147
Little Rock, AR 72221
info@siblingrivalrypress.com

Printed in the United States of America.

ISBN: 978-1-937420-75-8
ISSN: 2159-0478

Assaracus: Issue 15.
July 2014.

POETRY BY

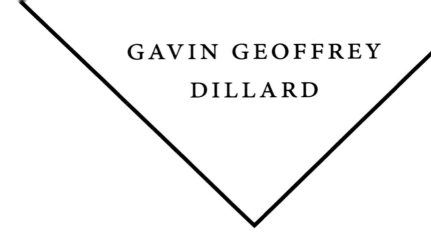

GAVIN GEOFFREY DILLARD

YOU WILL NOT BE YOUNG FOREVER

GAVIN GEOFFREY DILLARD has published eight collections of verse, two anthologies, and his infamous Hollywood tell-all, *In the Flesh: Undressing for Success*. Also known as "The Naked Poet," his poems have been recorded by James Earl Jones and Don Adams and have been published in anthologies and periodicals worldwide. Forthcoming are an opera, *When Adonis Calls*, comprised entirely of his poetry, and an anthology of his life's work, *The Mortal Poems (the first half-century)*. Many of Dillard's private letters, notes, and files were donated by Dillard to the Gay and Lesbian Archives of the San Francisco Public Library. He lives in North Carolina.

Q: Who are your poet heroes?

I have few contemporary heroes. Whitman and Dickinson are compelling for their journeys. Emerson and Tagore are both genuine masters. Millay wrote one brilliant poem. But my inspiration comes from ancient masters: Ono no Komachi, Izumi Shikibu, Bashō, Saint Francis, Saint John of the Cross, Rumi and Hafiz, Mirabai, and of course Lao Tzu; those who have actually touched God, and written about it, are my heroes. Everything else is just artifice.

IT IS DIFFICULT NOT TO IMAGINE HOW MY LIFE WOULD HAVE BEEN DIFFERENT. HAD I MARRIED IAN MᶜKELLEN.

Some years ago, in Santa Monica, my friends Chris and
Don had in mind to marry me off to the knave. It was on the
occasion of an art exhibit of Don's drawings and paintings of
their good friend, Sir Ian (then still a commoner);
Don had painted many a portrait of me as well, but fewer than
that of Ian. Ian was apparently out a husband and Chris was
convinced I should fit the bill nicely. Mr McKellen was not a
famous movie star at the time, but a renowned Shakespearean,
and an avid appreciative of poetry.
I was far from famous, but had my fan base and remained
published. The problem was that I was already romantically
entwined with a man far wealthier and more prizeworthy, who,
though hardly of a poetic inclination, was sexy in his own right and
by any reckoning an unqualified political coup.
I said no thank you. I came to the opening early, and
left before Mr McKellen arrived.

"Fate," "destiny" . . . these loaded words we tag serendipity and happenstance;
the will of God is irreversible and irretractable. Hindsight is
foresight and neither of use to the Poet.
Of course had I embraced the now-iconic Mr McKellen I would have
obliged him into the open much earlier, as I did my
Hollywood mogul. On the other hand, I might have
participated in the filming of the *X-Men* series and, more
importantly, Peter Jackson's superlative *Lord of the Rings* magnum
opus—without argument the greatest cinematic event of all time.
I might have been in both series, a mutant myself, an orc and
an elf. I might have pilfered dirty pairs of socks of both Hugh
Jackman and Viggo Mortensen. The fun might've been
beyond all imagining.

Instead I almost died in a one-room shack in the mosquito-
infested jungles of Maui, with no bath or running water, and only
enough power to boil my tea and run the computer from which I
penned infinite pages of haiku about being a lonely and desolate monk;
I parted with Hollywood and took to the hills, studying with
a host of arcane gurus and yogis and awaiting the end of the world.
My world indeed ended. And so it began. I now host a wee
tea plantation in Appalachia and write for classical
compositions. My career is surprisingly on course after
decades of stunning desolation. There are cats and men and
artists in my life like never before. My gurus now
treat me as an equal—more importantly I treat
myself as an equal—and I am privy to silences rare
among the world of men.

A wizard should know better. But a poet knows that
perfection exists in the smallest of things, and that the
choices we pretend we make are eternal;
I am old now, older that Sir Ian was then, and yet, as I
watch and rewatch the Tolkien epics, I think how
differently it all might have been. Had I
      married Mr Gandalf.

ANDREW

From the first glance, I was
butter melting down his chin,

through the beard, now
lost in the dense forest of his
breastly dell,

where all I hear is the
beating of heart—

whether his, or mine, I
cannot tell.

FOR FATHER JAMES (AND ZACHARY QUINTO)

If I became a suicide bomber for Christ, do you think
God would give me Zachary Quinto in the next world?
Hell, I could go for a religion that
delivered!

Enough with limp-wristed Protestantism;
shit, even Satan is mute and without tooth.

And Zachary six million miles away,
in a town without a soul.

DEAD THINGS ALONG THE ROAD

Dead things along the road, strewn endlessly in
every direction. Cold, still, alone, some
broken, some merely frozen in place; wee furry beings that
once roamed the woods, then mistook a roadway for a
stoney meadow.
Many I recognize: coon, possum, skunk, fox . . .
others are strangers, with stripes and horns and
mythic designs; they are
us in every way.

I have died so many times along this road, at the hands of
careless drivers, drunks and hapless teens;
so many murders, so much blood, the enemy is
always on the move.
For one brief flash I was free and wild, at full trot, I was
living my life; for one precious moment I had
outrun the world, my sprint winged and
unencumbered.

We are chimera, puppets upon a stage, which
luckless lie limp and undriven; but oh, for the moment we
disgorge our lines, render our verse, sparkling
beneath those halogen eyes: we
transcend these huddled wads, we
soar with the owls,
and the places we travel are
nameless and eternal.

NOTES TO SOME YOUNG GAY FRIENDS

1. Although it goes against common wisdom, the fact is that not every older queen wants to get into your pants, no matter how cute you are. It's simply not a universal truth. So relax; deal with it.

2. Having not had the advantage of growing up before the dubious "liberation," I must inform you that you have been brainwashed. You do NOT have to be in love, have a boyfriend, have a lover, or get married and adopt 1.5 Chinese or African babies. This is not a requirement and will not make you complete. You can fly solo, you can be a slut or a monk, a crazy poet like me, or find an extended family of undefined borders. Get a pet, they're cheap and constant.

3. You will NOT be young forever. So use what you've got wisely. But USE it.

4. Be smart, be aware, be open, and aging will find you more blissful as every year passes.

5. Death is not a punishment or failure, it is a graduation.

6. Crazy is a positive attribute at any age.

RILEY

When next we encounter, remind me to show you the
photos of Mike Riley;

he was a photographer as well, we took endless
photographs, knowing that they would be
all we'd be left with.

These three years later, I found a roll that had slipped to the
bottom of the camera box, now developed and
printed; a refreshingly

unflattering collection, naked in the barn, the light
fracturing in at an odd angle, his face
uncertain—we had

most likely been fighting (always a safe bet) and the
angst quite apparent. I printed but one, a
portrait of Archimedes, our tuxedo

cat, gazing up at Riley's genitals—
his glorious gonads—

I dare say the finest junk I've ever seen or encountered
(mirrored only by his perfect smile).

It is the smile and the genitals that I most
recall—I hardly need photos—for the rest of
him now is much a blur;

but this is why we take pictures,
to capture the impossible,
and remind us of the parts we can't remember.

GAVIN GEOFFREY DILLARD

MEDITATIONS ON A THEME BY WILLIAM BLAKE:

Drive your cart and your plow over the bones of the dead.

> I bury my dead daily, in the garden, where the ashes
> nourish the seedlings of tomorrow's inspirations.

The road of excess leads to the palace of Wisdom.

> Once is rarely enough, thrice is nice;
> never waste an opened bottle;
> limits are for towns, countries, and mortals.

Prudence is a rich ugly old maid courted by Incapacity.

> I've never met Prudence but I've seen her
> husband, limp and wailing upon the dance floor, where
> even the nuns and maidens avoid his fearful,
> > hollow gaze.

He who desires but acts not, breeds pestilence.

> We are at least in part the sum of our experience;
> I would rather regret an action taken than an
> > opportunity missed.

Sooner murder an infant in its cradle than nurse unacted desires.

> Children are inquisitive by nature, experiential by
> default—in some small way they are their
> parents' desires, which still said parents seek to
> suppress; nay, murder the parents and let the
> child blossom:
> Truth lives in the open heart!

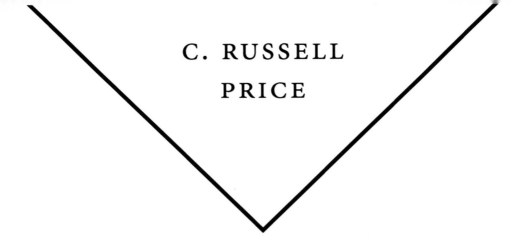

C. RUSSELL
PRICE

MOONBURN

C. RUSSELL PRICE holds a BA from the University of Virginia and an MFA from Northwestern University. Currently, Price serves as the Senior Poetry Editor of *TriQuarterly*. He teaches poetry to senior citizens in Chicago and plays pop piano covers in shady bars. Price is spending this year working on a directed collaboration between Chicago citizens to create a polyvocal, poetic novella via free writing workshops.

Q: Talk to your fifteen-year-old self. What would the poet you've become tell the boy you were?

Not everything you attract will be desirable. Just because a man is beside you doesn't mean you sh(c)ould love him. You're young; be wild and fucking fearless.

Q: Who are your poet heroes?

Frank "The Tank" O'Hara, Plath, William Carlos Williams, Alex Lemon, Tim Dlugos, Gregory Orr, Ingeborg Bachmann, Edna St. Vincent Millay, Tony Hoagland, Fiona Apple, Courtney Kampa, Christopher George Latore Wallace.

I LOSE MY VIRGINITY TO YOUR STRAIGHT BEST FRIEND AFTER YOU STAND US UP

Xanax and tequila
are the perfect mix
for us, for your soccer
shorts to come
off and on my floor,
for clotheslining
the kitchen table clean.

At two AM,
my neighbors pace
above you
inside me.

This is no
longer guilt
by association,
this is do not
tell, anyone, him,
the koi pond on the way
to work the next morning.

I wanted to lose
it to someone
unimportant, unsuitable
for a family funeral.

I wanted you
only for this poem.

THE POEM IN WHICH I PICTURE OUR HANDFASTING ORDAINED BY A MAN WHO MAKES POTIONS IN A TRAVELING SHOW

O, my little Lucille Clifton, my moonburn,
forgive me for leaving eyeliner on your earlobe
and for thinking us gods as we puddle

into the haybails that were once a queen
sized bed. A woman walks in—*not really*—and shines
her searchlight onto, first, your feet, then up, up, up

to your leg wrapped around each of my chipped vertebrae,
and that look I give you that says when you leave, I'll book
us two tickets: anywhere—

Albuquerque, Albemarle, Baltimore, Jacksonville—
the hillside covered in chiggers and briars
where I tasted my first White Owl

peach cigar—the Peep factory I'll buy for six seconds
of your beautiful face soft boiling, hungry, no
hungrier since birth for the castle I'll make from Arizona

Sweet Tea cans and canary jaws where we wait drinking
on lawn chairs, watering cowshit patties, watching for the cap
of this synced breath to pop through and bring us back

to this fixed rent Babylon where you wrap my emerald heart
in snakeskins and clover, where above our anastomosing
my neighbors are dressing for church, their hymn-hums

shake what bones of mine are left deeper into yours.

LA QUESTION C'EST VOULEZ-VOUS

Today, I made more curtains and asked you,
Paul, to wreck them all. "But dear," you said, "what
about the man in Mississippi you'll meet
in five years on a natural bridge between
two swampbogs, who once home in your
little shackatini by the roadside will say, *Russell,*
dear, we have matching swatches. Mr. Mississippi's
eyes will scurry up the seamline and even as he's speaking
about a needle's size, I think of the most beautiful phrase
Paul's ever said, "Double Bubble Cotton Candy Gum" or
his knack for mispronunciation or the small patch of skin
near the ribs that had the makings
to be a third nipple.

*

This unlucky city will be good
enough for a while, while I wait
for him to love me in the rosemary
hills that cover the riverwalk's shores
or in the tchotchkes, tchotchkes, tchotchkes
we bought and brought back from a smoky
Chinatown in a sweating August.

*

Tonight, his breath reaches out
of a taxi for the back of my neck
in a dimly lit Dykes-on-Bikes bar
near the Northside. Beer-mustached,
he leans in, the suds still settling
on his oyster mouth, and without warning

he drags me down through the pixie-cut
hedged human river to the dancefloor's pistil,
where around us the women petal
for two leather jackets dancing for the first time.

*

Everyone is wanting
this, even the Swedish band, ABBA, even the bull
pouring us another round, even the line near the loo
looks to his hand slowly vining up,
chasing away each stubble of my shadow.

POSTCARD: YOUR SECRET LOVER SARAH (WITH AN H)

I am myself and that is
not enough to keep
you, my fire ant mess,
another night from whomever
she is. She is
because you are gone
and my world crumbles
at the sound of her call.

Outside my window, you talk
to Sarah (With an H), cut yourself
off at two beers. What I would give,
a nut, to feel your Brillo Pad beard.
With all my tongues, I'd carve
an ampersand into your extra rib,
I would Dali wash your face,
my melting, golden pocket watch.

And once in her pussy-
palace of brownstone and gentrification,
does she smell the smoke I left
in places I did not touch?
Does she turn on herself
and slip into her fucksuit?

She's the *kind of girl* who owns
a rickety, oak headboard
just for all the noise
two bodies can make.

I want to say to her
you are the *kind of man*
who'll leave when his lover
gets plumper. How I've survived
on rice and spite, on this strange,
skyblue hunger for you,

how she should find me
when she starts naming
her dream-spawn, how I'll give her prints
of our antebellum home, our
three Hebrew boys,
how she'll know another she's come along.

POSTCARD: MY DRUG DEALER TAKES ME TO A GANGBANG ON GLENWOOD AVE

A party you'll appreciate,
he says, passing the White Widow
grape blunt which chimneys
the memory of fucking a blonde
in the southern college laundry room.
His mouth: the open washer,
the feeling of sack against white
dented doors. What does one wear
to a place, just to peel it all?
Like a hornet's nest, the men
beside me bareback.
The hallway smells of cat piss
and looking at the V-hips
moving, I imagine all the extra
organs my body has produced
since stripping my tank.
One man goes on break
and eats a cheeseburger
while his lover takes, and takes,
and takes. I am here,
and not, to only watch
the greasy finger push
the buzzer's button, the john
from the cream doorway
into a bed with too many
furry legs swishing, a cage
full of rabbits rutting.

GET BEHIND ME, SATAN

When you cut me off and out, seven hundred and seventy-five miles away,
I crawled into your letters and blue moons, your California cornflakes.

Inside the envelope, I couldn't find your white nurse or lost stardust,
behind the stamp, I whispered *baby, baby, baby* to crisscross the gluegum.

I carried six Arizona Sweet Teas and a pack of Kools through deserts
     to your door,
my boombox blasting The White Stripes: *thump thump, icky, thump thump.*

O Batman! O black pearl! Whatever you've been looking for in the snow,
blowing the world away with a bazooka, I don't need to see.

I'm telling you for the first and last time, your white horse is here,
without a Cadillac, but with simple syrup and every last bumblebee.

Wear whatever face you find, test each one for a week, break-in the noses,
I'll know you by your blinks, by the O only your mouth can make.

THE POEM IN WHICH PAUL DRIVES 13 HOURS
TO MY HOMETOWN, SOLO

You do not know that the limping man beside the butterfly
bushes is my Father, and passing him on the Tennessean sidewalk
he tips his ballcap. And were you close enough to see
if his hands still smell like leather? Did you thank him for giving me:
insufferable busted veins, raging hypochondria? Did he call
you *boy*, too?—did you, shocked at seeing me cloned and older—choke

down your Pal's sweet tea and Dip Dog chili bun? Did you
    notice your similarities
in table manners and barbaric finger licking, lip smacking,
    even your biceps
say, here—here is a man I should know.
And the woman whose hand he's holding catches your eye
and the lightness you left in Chicago bubbles up through this hippie
woman's braids and there is no denying it—having heard of one another

for long enough to know the trills of your voices, she brings you home
where I haven't been since seven where my grandmother is happy
where the trees haven't died where a whole caravan of runaway pets
meets you at the door, and licking your shoe sole they know
    we've been together.
I picture you on my childhood bed, a room of blue,
enablers everywhere, the paintings covering poorly patched

walls where I made my hand a wrecking-ball after the locker
room boys taped the only openly gay kid to fieldposts: the drawer
where with some cheap cardboard I made a faux bottom to hide the razor
and the perfect airplane bottles, the lighter, the pipe, the nude print-off
of a man just dressed in a jock gripping his cock giving you that dusty look.
And Saint Osmosis crawls out of a notebook I taped below
    the lowest bookshelf—

aging parents will not kneel to snoop. And you meet him,
    the man you replaced,
all bitter loose ends, all crowbar complications, and you do not
    know that telling me
you were there, a wave of Chicago trains comes roaring
and the urge to walk right out into the nonstop street,
to Kate Chopin the day—across the platform from me, a man stands
with his seven year old son who's still dressed in baseball accoutrement,
    the cleats

clack against the station's concrete and echo past the elevators
    and I find myself
puking in a crowd on Cinco de Mayo completely sober.
I have the learned the golden rule of cruelty.
In my Dad's rusted-over, robin's egg blue pickup, he hit me
    for the first time
after I said: *I hate this.* And his fist busted open my lips till the white
8 of my jersey glistened crimson on the fields of brick dust.

It has taken me 17 years
to forgive him, for the frustration he must have felt for the ghost
trophies, for wanting what is not in front of him.

I'LL TAKE YOU TO BERLIN TO GET RID OF THE BABY

Passing by the broken hearts growing
in the window boxes down Rosemont,
I miss you very little if at all.

A family of opossums crosses
the street after Church, and the father
says, "go ahead, it's only suffering."

When I reach the bar, the tender tender
recites, "You're waking empty/step back
from that ledge, my friend."

At the urinal, I piss-spell your name
and knock three times on the ceiling
and wander out to CVS.

What color, what shade to slide
up my sleeve? There's no *14. Y.O.
Texan Girl Who Just Got Dumped.*

Instead, I settle for *Onyx Rush
445* and the beep of please scan
your card shatters the Heart playing overhead.

Once home, I make myself a lady
busy writing thank you cards
while drinking whiskey from a mason jar.

The neighbors knock and want to join
in on destroying your everything
with a prescribed burning.

We open every window while the steel drum
crackles with acrylics dripping, poems smoldering;
we crank the speakers till the Jack ripples.

My room is an ash field
at the moment. The neighbors cling
to one another; they know

there has been a death. The dust
pan comes around the corner
and we say dark things to each other.

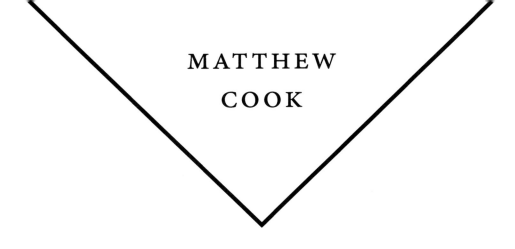

MATTHEW COOK

A SUBTLE CHAOS

MATTHEW COOK was educated at the University of California, San Diego and the University of Iowa. He earned his BA and was the recipient of the Stewart Prize at UC San Diego for his creative writing. He holds an MFA from the Iowa Writers' Workshop, where he was both a Maytag Fellow and an Alberta Kelly Fellow in Poetry. His work has previously appeared in *Squaw Valley Review*, *Penumbra*, and elsewhere. He has worked as everything from a legal researcher to a writing tutor to a barista. He is currently revising a full-length collection of poems. He is a poet who lives and works in Eugene, Oregon. Writing is how he goes home.

Q: What poem should we read aloud right now?

"For Matthew Shepard" by Dorianne Laux. It negates any labels while treating one of the greatest hate crimes of our time and positioning itself gently on the genderless beauty of love.

Q: What four people would appear on a Mount Rushmore of gay poetry?

Audre Lorde, Frank O'Hara, Adrienne Rich, and Walt Whitman.

PHYLLIS

At six I walked
in on my mother peeing,
her head pinned between
her hands. A miracle, I
thought. She wanted me
to see finished work
and sound meals
and not this. From the kitchen
she built a house around
herself, folding each one
of her husbands
into a clean apron.
Later she wore them
as jewelry. Sometimes
she was seven women
a day, sometimes less
than one. Husband three
preferred my bed to hers,
so she bedded with earplugs.
Mother does not hear
well now. Her shoulders
may read lips. Even when
she walks away she walks
towards me, I am of her,
and even if she does not,
I must remember the grace
between her legs, the unusually
warm afternoon in late
December when her
need touched mine
for the last time. Look
down at me, Mother.

COMMUTER FLIGHT

Invisible, ether mist will either
materialize into words or Dramamine.
My stomach is still confused.

I have passed over your house
fifty-seven times at two thousand feet.
Do you believe me?

Turbulence is coming,
and it will punctuate
this space into a hundred dips,
opening into hopscotch
and then sweetening willingly
into a waltz over the squared fields below.
The plane will have no time
to stretch its legs:
the atmosphere will lead
and the aircraft will follow.

The pilot announces that,
despite the weather, beverage
service will be provided.
"I will risk certain head-injury,"
says the stewardess, "for Coca-Cola."

The older man in front of me
audits the flight attendant—
our sudden sister—noting her precise,
prepared window of femininity,
so distant is she in her womanhood
he thinks only of his honey-roasted peanuts
and the lime in his gin.

The pilot in instructional voice-over,
explains, "Erica Jong is on the left wing.
Her class on orgasms, however,
will be cancelled." All passengers
groan with either disappointment
or misdirection.

Most people familiar
with an hour
would not recognize it here.

The air oxidizes
the scaffolding of measure
into mist, the metal skin
threatening to burn off like fog.

We've been hearing rumors
of a revolt in business class.
Commuter polls indicate
two out of three passengers
prefer word problems
to reading *War and Peace*,
even on an airplane.

The middle-aged woman
next to me reaches
through the window,
rubbing the moon for powder
and patting it gently on her nose.
She says, flatly, "You can't get
makeup this good through customs."
We all know she's right.

The wings culminate
into feathers, the metal
softens into down.
Mangoes three thousand
miles away grow succulent
and ripen, their spell now
gravity in the night air.
Pineapples shake their mighty hips,
coconuts snap to attention,
and pomegranates everywhere harmonize.
The airplane smoothly spins
from waltz into salsa
for just one dance.

We are circling, rolling,
hawk-diving and stacked,
now orbiting among other jets,
circling the rim
of a deep sapphire glass,
chinking and melting
as ice in a dark cylinder.

Every pilot thinks
it's roughly their turn.

The top of the long, rectangular box
clanks closed, the lights dim
along the walls, the metal case
drops vertically among
the blooming flowers of light,
and everyone you've ever met is watching.

LEFTOVERS

Either it is or it isn't: "Chutney is the ketchup
of Morocco," yields a nervous Portland chef.
The phrase arcs unopened through the auricle
to a battled lip across a candle wick
searing the palette onto a glitzy menu,
an uncivil scallop advancing, extinct it lectures
about unfolding, sauce, cooking babble,
a salted hook, a tall potted plant's fronds
hinged into a limbed taste. Leaving the restaurant
in twilight, the warps of leap, tonguing,
spore into substructure, follicles and glacial
migrations, a diaspora into the mouth
of relief, *home* into curry, the rear
of the kitchen, bauble of thought cascades
as I hunkered into the telecast of a breakfast nook
with a cat that never took to me—
what in a household would have been a kitchen,
the plastic bag and a can opener, tin
against steel, a tomato *jus*—vaulted slogans expanding
within insulated mush, the open receptacle
a monument, polished into the phantom
of landmark, paramount architecture of the past
confined to the one time you built dinner.
Its sun a closefisted orange,
watercolors caramelizing to night,
the splintered window of its lens
opening as an aperture into the way
light shifts and hardens out of the form
of a thing that is not.

AFTER ARTICHOKES

After you, in consideration
of my dusks, artichokes—
singular and unbroken
leaves stalked and strung
out into mulled afternoons,
I expected God would show up,
at home in the present tense, a first
person wrapping my throat
in sheets of white plastic,
teeth curling into giant white
pills I would swallow and say
all of the right things
so there would be no room
for this, the world falling
through a net of nomenclature
and produce, the draining
of your garden plants, the pit
of the backyard within the avocado
sunrise, the sky a vacuum sucking each leaf
out into space, biology a duologue
sifting through the clock,
hands chipping green into brown,
feet disintegrating through drifts
of sand, an hourglass slipping
out from beneath the mayonnaise
jar's shine, its tour from the cabinet
of headless pennies, glass cracking
under the pressure of summer's surface,
the tail of a dog flaming, panting and rabid
with the burn of July's final geology.

THE OTHER LIFE OF RAINFOREST EPIPHYTES

This morning on the freeway
my minivan started talking again.
"I feel so naked," it said,
"you know, sitting out there at night,
next to the garden, while you're inside.
I need a *God Rules* sticker to cover up."

I take my minivan more seriously
than most Christians in other sects,
or so I gather from the church.

The hood begins to turn
an even darker shade of red
against the haze of roadbed.
Shame is such a problem color:
nothing goes with it, but it does
get excellent gas mileage,
so I drive the kids out to the high
desert instead of school.

There, the night-blooming Cereus
provides the most concentrated
sense of calm, being one
of the better desert flowers.
It has been a dry season:
the sky near-white with its daystar
bleaching most parts of horizon.

The Cereus will wait until night,
wondering, perhaps, about its cousin,
Rainforest Epiphyte, a small hitchhiker
between the trees, drunk on water vapor

and a hemisphere away
from drought or discipline.

What would life be like in the forest?

I heard a story once that
natives dine on the night-bud,
their arms blooming easily
under the twilight.

I will continue the fast, a way
of going without. My wife
smells everything on my breath,
and this is one, in particular, she
would love to spot. "Ah ha! Jungle
food!" she would say.

Her cooking is exact,
every dish so precisely the same,
she only makes lone articles.

It has become so acutely bland,
yet I cannot stomach anything else,
for this is now all I am able to eat.

MATTHEW COOK

THE LAST DAY OF SUMMER

Soon the reflecting pools will refuse
to do their jobs, the ashes from urns
dissolving into weightlessness, lifting
into the sky and claiming the entire season.
Deep within seepage, order is beginning
to loosen itself, flooding all plateaus
with an unfolding rain of leaves. I keep
looking behind myself—over both bladed
shoulders: *Is there someone behind me, coming
down that path from the hills?* The Council
has placed a wanted ad, carving urgency
out into bedrock: *Sun God needed, apply
within.* So multiple the heroes, each dying
their symbolic death. Mother Jung, a high,
old culture elevates in the subterranean sea
of your breast—Nox is collapsing and a legacy
will feed. The stars speak a span of inversions—
Dionysus' replacements coming with the autumnal
equinox, evaporating pools of summer
until I am left standing displayed
and caked in sediment. From here I will
pray for the return of Prometheus, stealing fire
to bestow it again, giving these spayed forms
of tending, scarred in sex and printed
in flesh. Grapes will combust from their vines
in mid-winter, mountains loosening
into metaphors, rivers over running
and turning as leaden as lithe silhouettes.
I will for the first time in emergency reach
for another, seizing merely towels, soft,
but far too late to wipe the venom deadening
this rind.

THE BEACH HOUSE

I did swear on it. The Bible
was imaginary. Much of it remained
natty, every signature to every
signature, the least tuning. Particular
dubs tested a primitive breach, far-off
and animated, next agile: the approach
of some sharp and pinched form, maybe personal
revenge. Sunup snaps into the secret reader
of a strange book. It is often a relief to find much
of the world still here. Sundry and all divine
in the dim. Attic the mind's rank,
casting back much of a house, tracing a season
of salt on another earth. Windows are generally
as interested as fingers, ready to open onto an inner-aim
almost expressed. Preparing privately, I waited
to be brilliant without trying. The moon
ticked overhead while most crabs
fashioned new and larger shells,
waiting between rocks
to put them on, their meat
pulpous, dry and fitted
tightly to a tide.

LESSONS OF THE VULTURE

I am sick of nature,
its continuing. Sharks have
a memory of a minute or two.
They have to keep swimming,
even when they sleep. I rise,
force myself into morning.
Mountains and trees grin,
drunk on ocean. I have
the deepest thirst for salt,
a bodied bed, lying down.
A vulture dives and says:
I will not allow you hands
or a mouth until you
know what you mean.

THE ANTECEDENT DAYS

I am full of everything
except myself. There is some
tragic voice burning with table scraps
across the sky.

God is, notably, skipping
from house to house, selling
nearly perfect tamales.

More duties of genuineness
stumble to the other side
of the tracks. My brain is chapped
with fever and foresight.

Soon the world will flood
with brine, and some jail time
I did for shoplifting beads
to complete my rosary
may disqualify me
from the Ark.

My one shot
at *The Love Boat*
and I even fucked that up.

Even though the antecedent
days were swollen with zip,
I nevertheless want them back.
Call me and I will answer,
even if the name is not mine.

The *Valley of the Dolls* wasn't such
a bad place. At least the objectives
were clear. I used all of the toothpicks
from the avocado seed in the sill
and the kitchen has never been
the same.

Cousins on the coast tell me
laundry detergent has amassed
along the beach. The offshore islands
are purportedly churning like balled
underwear in the surf.

The world may be clean
and beyond me when it puts
all of its clothes back on.

MORNING SWEAT

I start to think. Over
a hundred miles north

Hollywood
rises, Deco
ashes hemorrhaging
inside their varnished, stair-stepped tombs, the metropolis

O'Hara's Turner,
buried in her silk robe,
still smoking after death. *Lana,*
where was the last place
you reached? Orchids across
the city shudder
in their phosphorescent vases.

A stardust
settles on the neon, a subtle
chaos

flickering out.

THE REST

In the neon lavatory
of the witching hour, the sky
computes the T-cells
of an old queen. The bleached bodies of scattered
suns stumble into the pouches
of black

holes. The day
will be no different except
there will be a sun
and maybe a bird

or two. There is half
pathos in his density, like the pink
letters in the sign: The "HILL"
part still there, the "C" fading
from fluorescence into darkness
and the "REST"

simply gone. He doesn't leave
his one
bedroom much. Before the valium
removes his head he observes:
My eyes are too much like memory.

THE GIFT

My mother is at the stove, distilling a tea kettle of flame.
She salutes, pouring until hunch unties cadaver, severance
of the whiplash tongue. Divorcing husband three,
life divorced her father. Sailing his tentacles
for the maiden, his pump fathomed, huffed, sank. Spun

of trade, little is alleged of the walls. Nails
where pictures wilted wipe up departure. Ear
nuzzled to the attic and it's goose eggs, loud
blood staying my frame.

Death has never been this available. Twenty-odd years
ago mother spliced off her hands, saddling me
to pose them over his military grave. They now iron his shirts
and he wears them, not because they are textbook,

but he would be otherwise naked. After my accident
she barked: "If I had hands I would bandage
your feet." I roughed, "You brought hell into this house
and now it surprises you?" After living wage at the table
she spent the kettle, torn-leave liquid proud despite her nipples.

The sun fell, the mountains
threw up stars. One faint light turned
and winked. My mother saw it, talked herself down,
as if the past were the only thing
that would keep happening.

And yet there is certain fitness, a plain and stealthy
sparkle to the envelope, the sure cleanness, pregnant
with nothing unless you choose to gorge into the floor
or through the ceiling. And the details are again perfect,
on the surface, where it counts.

THE FOSSIL WALL

More often now my father feels
them, pockets of air opening, lazy then
half-winking windows around
the edges of yellowing circumstance.

The hibernating are beginning
to awaken in the space
behind corners of the present, inflating
old clouds, ironing out buckled parts
of sky: lives lived on sides
other than these.

A hand might soon well reach
through, rippling the glue of an ordered,
fossil wall and wave: *There is
so much more going on here.*

DAN ENCARNACION

MANHOODED

DAN ENCARNACION earned an MFA in Writing at the California College of Arts and lives in Portland, Oregon, where he co-curates the Verse In Person poetry series. The bleak of Béla Tarr, the spare of Supersilent, and the spike of quad-lattes will palpitate his palpus. Dan has recently been published in *Margie, Eleven Eleven, Exquisite Corpse, Berkeley Poetry Review, Five Fingers Review, SPLIT, Upstairs at Duroc, Cha: an Asian Literary Journal,* and elsewhere. He was the featured artist for *Reconnaissance Magazine*'s 2013 issue. His poem "Aposiopesis" was nominated for the 2014 Pushcart Prize.

Q: Who, writing today, excites you?

In fiction: Haruki Murakami, Robert Coover, László Krasznahorkai, Sjón. In poetry: Brian Teare, Alice Notley, Jack Gilbert, Frank Bidart.

Q: What four people would appear on a Mount Rushmore of gay poetry?

Walt Whitman, Thom Gunn, Frank O'Hara, and Gerard Manley Hopkins.

THE MEN

the men—knowing somebody is waiting—park a block away,
down the street, around the corner, in the cul-de-sac near
the flaccid aluminum-sided house littered with sere leaves,
sticky snack wrappers, and optimistic plastic toddler play-
paraphernalia turning black in the dust from car exhaust
billowing through a cyclone fence encapsuling the weed-
wedged yard from the freeway ramp declining less than
a gray football field away

knowing somebody is waiting—the men swing through double
metal doors and scan the room for the racks of naked women
frozen in gaping, gazing, waiting poses indifferent on glossy
covers of magazines and videos, seeking a space where they
can glean a leering view of the dvds and glossies exhibiting
naked men frozen in gaping, gazing, waiting poses indifferent
in humming fluorescent exposure, so that they may peek at
those men who hold the temerity to leaf through these bold
compromising poses in front of us unknown

the men scan these men for manliness—a formulary face of
masculinity—for discrete discretion, for willingness—horniness
is moot, if they're there, they are—for a shard of surreptitude,
for arrows that don't quiver for flight beyond lust and longing,
for similitude; the men scan these men for the convention of the
gay man who strives to seduce the straight man (per vaudeville,
the straight man is always the butt of the joke); the men hope
these men will buy a pocketful of tokens and slip into the dim
peristaltic, Kafka-kian corridors of the video arcade booths
breathing in the back of the store and wait

with more men like themselves, the men park their selves
in the tight dark halls of the labyrinthine video arcade pacing,
peering, posing, preening, feigning indifference—a palliating
rake of their psychomachistic heads—passively wanting, but
waiting, reprobatedly waiting for the other to market contact—

with a slippery eye, a door left indicatively ajar, invite him
inside, hook the latch, drop the tokens, flip on a man-woman
fuck flick, press up against him with strategically exposed
skin lit by the monitor screen that scours every inch with
a subaqueous, glacial blue

he has dropped his tokens so you must drop yours; should
you look in his eyes what would you see but the ice blue
luminance of the fuck video reflected and maybe him
glancing back to pin your trespass; you note the shine
of his nose, his licked lips serious and wonder if he is one
to kiss; hands busy, skin unhid—clothes drape binding
spontaneous flight; you bite his nipples and you hear
his voice and it does not dismay you and you discover
you're on your knees before he—his tumidity you engulf;
you hear him refraining—try to hold himself back; you
surmise that he felt no intrigue, no attraction; you were
merely a man

the men depart thinking of allocated spaces outside anonymous
office buildings collegiately-clustered, aswim within immaculate,
raked berms, languorous alongside periphrastic thoroughfares
that snake from cloverleaf ramps funneling out freeways flying
over gray pigeon-shit sidewalks and syringe-strewn playground
sandboxes; causeways that cross and counter and jab and clutch
to enable the men to pass unseen to that parking space, down
that block, down that street, around that corner, in that cul-de-
sac where sleeps that aluminum-sided house with that play-
paraphernalia turning black in that car exhaust billowing through
that cyclone fence encapsulating that weed-wedged yard from
that freeway ramp declining less than a gray football field away

the men depart thinking there will always be somebody
to wait for them

CHILD

His hand is just something to grip
- Christopher Isherwood, A Single Man

Walking through the carpark I find your body just
Outside my line of vision your body not like you at
The rosary where you flushed face buried beneath
A mortician's hopeful palette as if embarrassed by
Your spotlit place no you're standing next to a shear
Wall dapper in a fine-cropped beard smoking a Kent
Looking pensive looking numbed looking away red
Tip embering out the shadows left hand fisted solidly
Down in your pant pocket the awkward acceptance-
Emptied well-meant little boy seared behind thick
Cheeked premature hair that let that faceless man
Fuck you fuck you a faceless man in a porn store
Fucked you holed up in a tissue-sotted video booth
Came unto you came into you your whole heaving
Into your ear it was your face your blood-flushed
Face eyes veined raw with poor regret ten years
After that I stared at daggered when you told me
But was the cached catching voice of the fumbled
Hung, ied intentioned boy that rose to say that after
He pulled out he whispered to you as you caught
Your breath and wondered if your ass would snap
Back to shape wondered if the burn would soothe
Wondered if he would do more to you anything
More so you could get off too content a man said
Fevered you thought *I will never leave you alone*

The elevator stops at a floor not lit up on the inside
Panel the doors slide back and nobody is there in
The shine of the fire extinguisher hung in the hall
I find a frail recollection of your face your face still
Bearded van dyked a reflection that slowly includes
All of you hands down in both pant pockets bending

Over reading the instructions for proper extinguisher
Use like the meticulous inquisitive optimistic ten year
Old boy that won first prize at a state science fair and
In that hallway your manhooded ghost melts into that
Optimistic meticulous inquisitive boy beaming bright
Braced teeth in that browned photo you brought me
Of your scientific success the catching voice that spoke
For the frantic shaky pallid man that read instructions
In their extent to escape eye contact the catching voice
That asked the nurse at the clinic whether a person
Could catch HIV swallowing cum because you couldn't
Admit an unfaced man fucked you fuck you you let
Someone you never saw fuck you

A Christian testimony transistors through the wall from
The kitchen next door the one with a wife with sallow
Eyes anxious stray a husband self-denyingly husband
Of gestures incorrigibly fey a rapturized voice pillowed
And pinched by insulation and pipes pontificates about
The beneficence of God glories in yielding to God and
Gives thanks to God for how He had directed it to the
Only affordable doctor who could help its palsied
Son I hear the catching voice of the earnest loyal
Conscripted altar boy a voice that I heard nightly and
Each Sunday seep through the phlegm of a shaven
Evaporating man a catching voice that made me turn
Face the outside edge of the bed the catching voice
Of the conscripted earnest loyal altar boy once spry
And sunny now spilling and spattering asking God if
The medication he had read about was really going
To be available for the sick to use a caught voice that
Asked God if getting AIDS was a punishment or just
An indication that his purpose on earth was complete
The loyal earnest conscripted altar boy who comforted
Himself that if his purpose on earth was complete then
His purpose must have been to love me a man voided

Of compassion to buff off my tarnish to help me clarify
Cleanse my life to ground me guide me to illuminate
My path towards some sort or other of yes spiritual
Transport yes your purpose was to love me because
He fucked you you once had said

I feel the catching voice of the meticulous intentioned
Loyal constricted boy I feel it earnestly fumble down in
Me but cushioned by folds of seclusion I feel it vibrate
In my throat as I lie in bed an exhausted voice I catch
Ask each passing night why he's gay if it's punishment
Or just a symptom that life would necessitate living
More self-consciousness than most

THE VILLAIN

THE STEREOTYPE IS A POLITICAL FACT, THE MAJOR FIGURE OF IDEOLOGY.
- ROLAND BARTHES, THE PLEASURE OF THE TEXT

And he lumbers rotundily up the slender street
From firm calves—a low of geniality, a draft of tractability
Alas, to glimpse his face—perchance, to meet

To be his socks that pillow, that swathe his feet
That cinch his stout Achillean insecurities
May you lumber unbeset upon upon the slender street

Brow made tame with locks salted discreetly epicenely chic
My hunger pinned by your gluttonous propensities
Alas, to sate your face—perchance, to meet

No doubt, no doubt, a maiden you would entreat—
To cast off your boots, air out your toes—grained with a taste for piety
After you should lumber rotundily up the street

Large lupine ears—all the better to hear, my sweet
Your thighs stride purposefully, pistoning plump cheeks
Alas, to kiss your face—perchance, to meet

You have much to offer
Evocative in your aggregated insulation against insularity
What have you to hide
The reason for your rhyme?

When does speculation become surfeit
My latte slinks bitter—punctuating singularity
Alas, he's lumbered up the slender street
Unlash my gaze, ungird your grace—perhaps

A CHESTERFIELD, FORGOTTEN
"*. . . , ALL PURPLE AND BUDDING.*"
- *ITALO CALVINO, "THE HOUSE OF THE BEEHIVES"*

FOR PATRICK ADIARTE: SINGER, DANCER, ACTOR, FILIPINO

Less loud than the step of a mantis or a cleric of clouds;
Steeping tea; the tug of a shroud. More pale than the flash
Of half-phased moon you pass glowing through your undraped,
Uncleaned, unopened windows unlit above thin streetlamps.
More pale than the grapple of cold ocean foam beneath
Another's moon. As brisk as a drag of dried leaves; a bullet
Fingered and weighed; a spider web-weaving. A Chesterfield,
Forgotten, to burn. You've risen to dance with the man
You will marry and father me. Max Factored lips and a bun
Bound to be undone by the man you will marry and father me.
A Chesterfield quenched as brisk as a slipping heartbeat. Less
Loud than a wrinkle's vein. More pale than your face when
He fathered me.

Wah Kee was the name of the Chinese restaurant my father
Always took us to when he thought it was time for a change.
My mother wove my fingers around my chopsticks for proper
Balance then showed me how to apply appropriate pressure
To manipulate the tools into picking up and placing my morsels
Where I pleased. She said in China it is polite to slurp the soup.
She laughed when I first intentionally tried to slurp—my soup
Dribbling down my chin. A subtle, but bodied laugh; her red
Lips would open; peeking out from behind, her small straight
Teeth tinged nicotine dun. Whenever we went to Wah Kee,
And only at Wah Kee, I would slurp purposefully, mustering
Variance in my verve; she would always laugh, always with
Her same signature gravity.

My father taught me that change was playing the same three
Keys on the piano in different order, in different time. She
Taught me not to try to eat rice from a plate using chopsticks.
"Look around," she said. "At the Chinese. See how they eat?
It's not sensible to pick up rice with chopsticks. Rice is eaten
From a bowl. You bring the bowl to your bottom lip and push
The rice into your mouth. You can't fully appreciate rice if you
Eat it as individuals. It won't have any flavor." She asked the
Waiter for bowls. Pleased, he squeezed out a larger, more
Sincere smile. "It's alright to look around you. Sometimes,"
She said. "You can learn more by seeing with your own eyes
Rather than by resigning yourself to be taught."

I held the bowl close to my lip and felt the sticky grains fall
On my taste buds as I slowly slid a wad of rice towards me—
The plastic prongs rubbing along my tongue feeling as if
A dentist were probing my mouth. My mother continued,
"The man who invented chopsticks was ingenious. They work
As one when in your hand. When waiting to be used, they're
Separate, equal and aesthetically elegant. When stashed
Away with others, when needed, you can pick up any two—
They're interchangeable. And if you don't have any, you can
Easily use any two sticks as substitutes." My mother stopped
Talking, confident that I was managing my food smoothly
And occupied with deliberating over her insights regarding
Other peoples' approaches to bringing food to one's mouth.

My mother turned to attend to my father. He fingered his
Tea cup like a thimble—as if appraising its shine, assessing
Its depth, gauging its width, weighing its heft, conjecturing
Upon the efficacy of its force should he determine it to be
A projectile. She fed herself some rice—her eyes upon his
—Slid more egg foo young onto her plate, then mine. He
Looked up to see her suck some grains from out her teeth.
They contemplated one another. I looked straight ahead,
Into the empty place-setting across from me. We always

Had one too many people to savor the snugness of a table
For two. We were always one short to sate a table for four.
My parents would invariably sit across from one another.
While waiting for the food to arrive, my mother searched
My father's face and he would investigate the to-go menu
Tucked under the glass table top. He would read off some
Dish he'd be wary to try, then say that next time he ought
To try it to be different. He would forget what he had said
That next time we would find ourselves at the Wah Kee.

He would light a cigarette and she would watch him smoke.
I would concern myself with the black and white tv running
Behind the cash register counter, its volume turned way low
To be heard only by the owner's teenage daughter who spent
Her evenings doing homework between tabulating orders.
I've come to associate the sharp chiming of registers, their
Rigorous rattle as they totaled then flung open their drawers
With the silent-eyed girl who dropped change and fortune
Cookies onto our check trays.

The Hullabaloo dancers were shimmying and twitching sleek
In bright white outfits before a brooding Batman backdrop—
Broad black wings umbratic over their vestal revelry, antipodal
To their frenzied froth; a gelid visage isolate above the cape.
My eardrums stretched their skins to catch the faint strains
Of *Na-na-na-na-na-na-na-na-na-na! Na-na-na-na! Batman!*
From across the room, as if seizured sprites, the dancers flit.
The monochrome screen bleached the brown face of the one
Asian dancer to blend undifferentiatedly among the Caucasian
White faces of the other bacchants—instinctively, I knew it was
Him: his movements just a little bit more sharp, just a little
Bit more snappy than the longer-limbed others. The owner
Appeared at the register and switched the channel. No flinch
From his solemn daughter as she knew her priorities did not
Revolve around the television. A curl-coiffed round head—
Through the screen shone Peter Lorre's greasy air affecting
The ponce of an exotic, effete Asiatic in lubricious pursuit of
The Maltese Falcon. "Gardenia," slipped Spade's secretary
As Spade sniffed the scented business card. "Quick, darling!

In with him!" he blurted excitedly. And, thus, entered Lorre,
Nattily ungloving his hedonist's hands. He perched fondling his
Cane in a manner intimating the tip toe of—what I'd later learn
To be—deft fellatio; unfearingly fronting Bogart's hard gaze.
Lorre pulls a gun and Bogart's Spade knocks it away, snatches
Lorre's bantamweight wrist and, with it still in grip, dragoons
Lorre to punch himself with Bogart's middleweight vitality—
Lorre's Joel Cairo lay cold-cocked limp on Spade's firm couch.
Upon his recovery, he maneuvers to a mirror hung on the wall,
Seeks solace in the glow of his own brazen face. Lorre's hands
Fuss his rumpled shirt. I looked at my tawny hands—fingers
Gripping the grip my mother had woven into my chopsticks.
I looked at the Chinese people enjoying their food around me
—Rice bowls held to lips, chopsticks furiously levering grains
Into their mouths. I looked at the soberness of the owner's
Daughter. Am I of them? Am I a Hullabaloo dancer; a poncy
Peter Lorre; am I of my mother?

There was once an instance when I witnessed my mother in
A state where she was irrevocably livid with emotion. It's not
Easy to imagine the movie-musical *My Fair Lady* inflaming
Unadulterated anger, but when she caught me watching it
One afternoon on tv, her voice raised to a rasp that stung
My spine. From the doorway to the kitchen, she screamed
As if she couldn't bear to consider acknowledging the movie
By walking into its glowing presence. "That is a preposterous
Film! Ridiculous and insulting! Singing and dancing about
A dirty street whore made respectable by two queer old men
With more money than they can shove in her cunt!" I peeped,
She sells flowers, Mom. "A euphemism! A euphemism! It's
All a hypocratic code. People can't talk openly about whores.
If you discuss them, you dignify them!"

Smoke dreams from smoke rings, while a Chesterfield burns.
Max Factored lips, your bun bound to be undone, your seat,
Vacated, still radiating your defatigable heat. The cigarette
Has shriveled, incinerated to a red-stained stub. The table
Empty save for sweating glasses, half-filled; paper napkins,
Wet-ringed. The plush voice of Perry Como wafts through

Your vacancy—dissipating sleepy, snaking coils of smoke.
The void at the table, that watched your Chesterfield fizzle,
Watches you dance with the man you will marry and father
Me. With his cardigan tongue, he said you were *fetching.*
I keep yearning for you through smoke dreams. From smoke
Rings that old feeling returns.

This is the best, Chesterfield—And the time to change, today.
A—always milder. B—better tasting. C—cooler smoking.
"Always Buy Chesterfields" Perry Como says. *"They satisfy."*
Like yourself, the man you will marry and father me learned,
From Perry Como, that the mildest cigarette is a Chesterfield.
Can you deny the verity of a man whose smile could illumine
A cavern from gloom, whose voice could caressingly defrost
A frozen roast? The tempo turns. Other dancers' tripping
Feet increase. You roll your hips to "Papa Loves Mambo".
He goes to, she goes fro; He goes fast, she goes slow; He
Goes left 'n' she goes right; (Papa's lookin' for Mama, but
Mama is nowhere in sight); uh! A rope of limp ash slinks into
The ashtray you've forgotten. It weakens, then crumbles.
Your seat no longer radiates your heat. The man you have
Risen to dance with then marry and father me mambos with
Fury, bound to be undone, buried by a cloak of demureness,
Like me. He would be the one you keep.

My mother had smoked with the vigor of a Hoover vacuum
—*It beats as it sweeps as it cleans.* There are photos of her
From before she met the man who would be my father.
Black and white photos showed her skin so white against
The dark walls and barbooths that elaborated her contrast.
Color photos exposed her lips always a luscious, just this side
Of lascivious, red; her skin creamier than the hard, made-up
Face she later lit up; her blue eyes skinned, but swift incising.
Unless she is posing with her parents, she is unfailingly seen
Smoking—puckering release or anticipating a drag. As much
A part of her cellular structure as her attached earlobes—
A bit of my inheritance from her. She wore large button clip-
Earrings to shield her fragility—this before she met the man
Who would father me. After him, it no longer mattered.

Catch a falling star and put it in your pocket, never let it
Fade away. Catch a falling star and put it in your pocket,
Save it for a rainy day. Less loud than a stone in a brook.
After she met my father, she stopped smoking. It was hers
To stop. The man who would marry her and father me, he,
Like Perry Como, inhaled two and a half packs a day. She
Decided smoke was one thing she would not share with
This man. I started to smoke soon after my understanding
Of sex developed and I first noticed the stoic daughter of
The Wah Kee. There aren't any photos of myself puckering
Release or positioning my hand to drag or letting a lit stick
Shrivel gripped between my knuckles. Cigarettes would not
Define me. My youth was spent batting smoke. It was a
Nod to the dehydrating haze that coated the coruscating
Constellations of my childhood dim. When I first found the
Photos of my mother's smile—the frozen moments of before
She met the man who would father me, her smile bold and
As relaxed as her Chesterfield flaring from her right hand,
A finger, raised—I stopped smoking. It was hers.

THE MIND IS ITS OWN PLACE, AND IN ITSELF
CAN MAKE A HEAV'N OF HELL, A HELL OF HEAV'N

- JOHN MILTON, PARADISE LOST, 1:254-255

This poem contains lyrics from the songs: "Batman Theme" (by Neal Hefti), "Smoke Dreams" (by John Klenner, Lloyd Shaffer, Ted Steele), "Papa Loves Mambo" (by Al Hoffman, Dick Manning, Bix Reichner), and "Catch A Falling Star" (by Paul Vance, Lee Pockriss).

JEREMY
HALINEN

I MAKE OF YOUR BOWEL A HIVE

JEREMY HALINEN is cofounder, former coeditor, and current editor-at-large of *Knockout Literary Magazine*. His first full-length collection of poems, *What Other Choice*, won the 2010 Exquisite Disarray First Book Poetry Contest. His poems' most recent anthology appearances include *Gay City Anthology 5: Ghosts in Gaslight, Monsters in Steam*. Other poems of his appear in journals such as *Cascadia Review* (which published his queer erasure of T. S. Eliot's poem "The Waste Land"), *Cimarron Review*, *Court Green*, *The Los Angeles Review*, and *Sentence*. He delights and meditates and plays his piano surrounded by his beloved paintings and plants in a vintage Seattle apartment building that was first a brothel.

Q: How has being an editor informed your work as a writer?

It's taught me that revision is often the most exciting and rewarding part of the writing process.

Q: Who has most moved you at a poetry reading, and why/how?

Theodore Enslin (1925-2011), in I think September 2001, with the wind in his voice and the many musical/textual variations of his poems.

CAGE

FOR JONATHAN WILLIAMS, IN MEMORIAM

How the moment the bars seemed most solid,
least a mirage, and the lock, unpickable,
I'm still a person, I think, I thought, cagey,
irresolute—and surely someone would have
said yes, had I asked. We never said goodbye;
like two fireflies that at night, to two men
drinking whiskey on the rocks, seem awhile
not what they are but helicopters lurching, uncannily,
above distant hills, we were the whiskey
in each glass, we were the rocks, receding,
diluting the whiskey, the blood in the men,
we were closer, more fragile, than we thought.

POINT OF VIEW

They've just had sex, but now,

beside you,

they're standing in the pool,
kissing,
beginning,

missing
nothing.

One's arm and shoulder:
inked: smoke-gray grandfather clock

older than time; the other's cock still
stalling—

half past nine
or half past two, depending . . .

—his lover's, alas,
at half mast,

wavering
toward the water.

*

I notice most not moving
matter I can see

but sound I can't:
patterned rise and fall

of fractal moans

men host, the rainfall patter
of ejaculate,

that shattered, holiest ghost.

COMMUNION

Some men prefer it after dark,
a chain-link fence between them
their only protection. A fence
is but an idea of a border.
True borders need no fences
but are their own embodiments.
Together his beard and mustache frame
his lips, his tongue, my cock.
A cock is but another tongue,
fluent in many tongues, a bell-
ringing border crosser seeking
the center of someone to know.
An anus is not only the body's gate
but a portal to eternity rejoicing
in mortal form. Some fuck beside
barbwire fences to portray
pain's proximity to love.
Others fuck to wake the god inside
the other and worship, their twin
cumshots fallen angels rising
in unison, true and welcome.

RAW HONEY IN HAND

. . . HE TURNED ASIDE TO LOOK AT THE LION'S CARCASS.
IN IT WAS A SWARM OF BEES AND SOME HONEY, WHICH
HE SCOOPED OUT WITH HIS HANDS AND ATE AS HE WENT
ALONG.
- JUDGES 14:8-9

I make of your bowel
a hive

alive with a fistful
of stickiness,

safe haven for loot
of the sweetest

persuasion. Persuasion, which
it did, after all, take

to turn
your aversion

into avarice, get you
to let me split

your body like
the water of a lake

or the carcass of a lion
lying beside it.

May every sting you feel
be short

but sweet, like the cherry-
blossom dreams

of honey bees dying.

ANAL SEX IN HEAVEN

I'd rather a woman call me God
and rape me with a barbed-wire strap-on
than this, God's monster cock
pounding me from behind,
his hands groping me like ghosts'
in this attic where I'll gain nothing
miraculous
if he seeds my insides,
no son to birth: my name's not
Mary. Will it feel more like snow
or rain? I know: when he's about to spill,
I'll open up so wide
he'll fall right through me!
What's a little more pain?

FISTING THE DEARLY DEPARTED

takes a love that knows no
bounds, a curious blend
of charity and selflessness. What
is the measure of a man's
success? Pleasure wrought
after death? The wingspan
of a hand that, buried, finally
can fly? What comfort to discover
inside us is mostly sky.

I WILL NOT FIST YOU

while you sleep. You
have my hand, you
have my word. If you
should wake before you
die, I'll hum you
another lullaby. You
need not fret, you
need not cry, I ♥ you
even with my hand outside you.
What would you do if you
were a lake, if you
held my hand inside you
as beside myself I lay beside you
watching you
rippling, you
the cool wet, you
the stars' mirror, you
slowly freezing, you
and me with you.

PSALM

My man is my fister,
I shall not go empty.
He fists me beside the swimming pool,
he restores my hole.
He guides me through tunnels
of pleasure;
he's famous like that.
Even though I balk
at the thought of death,
I will know no fear,
for you are in me;
your fist and your wrist,
they calm me.

You move your hand inside me,
a gift given in secret,
stroke my cock with your other hand
until it flows over.

Surely beauty and grace will fill my days:
a man's hand
gentle beyond understanding, our joy
rippling into the universe.

ON FISTING

You don't really know anyone forever
until you've fisted them. That's a dangerous
word, *forever*, and a dangerous place to be
with anyone, so don't fist just anybody.
Don't be afraid to be choosy. Fuck 'em first
to get familiar with the territory.
If they're too tight or too loose or something
doesn't smell right, move on. It's ok.
This is America. They'll get over it
or a gun. You may have to run, but you'll
be free, and it won't last forever.

THE MERCHANT OF ANUS

is trying to sell me an anus.
I'd like to say I'm not surprised,
but I'm surprised I'm asking him
to lower his asking price
and if I might find the Merchant of
Gerbils nearby. You can lead a horse
to a puddle, you can
give a dog a plastic bone,
but an anus wants what an anus wants:
a homesick homely gerbil making it a home.

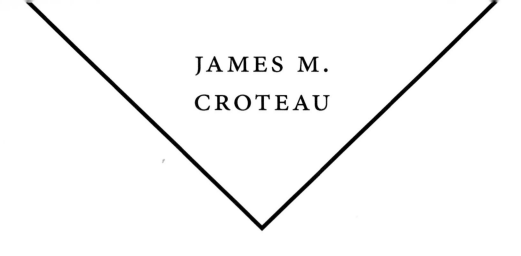

JAMES M. CROTEAU

ONCE TWO BOYS

JIM CROTEAU lives in Kalamazoo, Michigan, with his partner of 29 years, Darryl, and their two Labrador retrievers. He grew up gay and Catholic in the southern United States in the 1960s and 70s and has spent his adult life in small non-coastal cities. He loved his mother very much. He began writing poetry two years ago—at first to cope with life in times of aging. Then, well, he sorta caught the poetry bug. He is a professor of Counseling Psychology at Western Michigan University. Of these poems, "Evan," reprinted here, was previously published in the November 2012 postcard issue of *HOOT: a postcard review of {mini} poetry and prose*. Other work has appeared in *New Verse News* and *Right Hand Pointing*. He blogs about writing at talkingdogsholymen.blogspot.com.

Q: Talk to your fifteen-year-old self. What would the poet you've become tell the boy you were?

It will "get better," but will never fully heal. The scars are poetry fertilizer. You were brave and beautiful despite what you often still think.

Q: What are you currently reading and what have you learned from it?

I fall in love with novels that leave me emotionally vulnerable—a good state for writing poetry. Right now it's And the Dark Sacred Night *(Julia Glass).*

RISEN

Today I sit in sacred space
for queers, among gay boys
who rose from coffins
constructed in churches
of our youth and shake
my head at the familiar
feel of smooth oak.
In pews like these

I learned Jesus hung,
bloodied on the wood, died
to save me from the sheets
I stained at night, longing
for the red-haired boy
who lived across the street.
Each morning after came
the smuggled wash cloth
and a vow to disavow
further thoughts of Ben,
his red hair, his pale skin.

But good Catholic boys
abide by resurrection's rules,
three days later, I'd dream
the freckles on Ben's face
graced places on his body
I would never see.

COVER BOYS

In appreciation of Walt Whitman's
"Two Boys Together Clinging"

Each June yields his boyish grin,
his familiar smell of summer sweat
and well-tilled soil, my lover's harvest
adds to our table, his hands hold
sturdy stalks of green, paler
than the earthy headed horde
of fine florets. We clean and chop
this first crop, as we have each year
for thirty-six. The pot sets to boil,
steam fills the air with souvenirs—

we were once two boys together
clinging, I was there at his first
sight of ocean, we pledged in public
when marriage was a far horizon.
For all life's vigils we've held hands—
when time necessitated the vet's needle,
free hands on fur, we bid farewell.
Two boys by the sea, cover photo
for our album, almost filled, near forty years,
now we take pills with morning coffee,
two men aged together. The ring
of the kitchen timer, we do not cling,
turn off the burner, not much left to do

before we eat, add a pinch of salt
and a touch of butter. Half-a-smile,
half-a-joke, my lover says: *Picture us*
on the cover of The Advocate
or Out Magazine: Two old men
at their kitchen counter, bowed
over bowls of broccoli,
essential nutrient, home-grown.

ONE MORNING AFTER YEARS TOGETHER

More than a few snooze cycles are needed to get my lover out
of bed, this morning is no different with six repeating bouts of
buzz then quiet. Then I hear his rustling and look down to the
kitchen from the loft where I've been at my early morning writing
stint. He's standing at our kitchen counter, holding in his palm a
pale orange oblong pill, lisinopril. He opens sleep puffed lips and
swallows this marker of our bodies' slow decay. His snug white
jockeys snag my sight—I'm twenty again when we first made
ourselves inside each other. I'm down the stairs hugging him from
behind, but before lower bodies brush, he pulls away mumbles
morning, walks up the stairs, and shuts the bathroom door. The
shower's wistful music sounds right above my head. With each
change in rhythm, I hear his body being touched.

SKIM AND WHIP AFTER TWENTY YEARS

Use of years dulls the paring
knife, as apt to injure
finger as peel fruit.
So we whetstone a date night,
seek an angle and the coarseness
that'll put our edge back on.
The Common Grounds is half-way
between my office and his gym,
he's already ordered, his skinny,
my mocha caramel, predictable.
I sit, he sips, we know
if words venture he subdues,
if talk treads light, we know
my yawn. All terrain
seems off the table,
where our skim and whip
sit silent as we search.

AN ODE TO RANDY SHILTS AND PAUL MONETTE

You screamed your stories
from coastal cities—
one hot summer in 1979
in the flat Mississippi Delta,
I plugged one ear,
cupped the other,
and first heard you.

In these information-rich, gay-
marriage times, I want the young
to know the wonder
that was your voices,
the rich stories that made my life
real. You wrote me well
in a world that shaped me sick.

At 22, I read your book:
I was that boy in Minnesota
who called Harvey Milk,
many were, dear men,
you made our conduct becoming, declared
us mayors of our streets, guided us
in becoming men—
all in only half a life,
dead in the holocaust
you chronicled. Now I'm older

than you ever were, just past the brink
of summer, so to speak. I turn
again to search your words
for ways to live when it's too clear:
we all live on borrowed time,
all wait the last watch of night.

TILES THAT BIND

Boy feet felt the coolness
of the white, black, and beige,
subtle texture in each tile,
the sharper lines of grout;
sameness daily underfoot, promise
of solid ground giving float
to ships of childhood play,
an ocean's vastness in a simple tub.

Broken bits of beige and black, here
and there at fifty-five, tiles
underfoot one last time, extended
arms above the age-stained sink;
duty to dispose the dozen bottles
with mother's name, pack up
childhood's shelter, surrender
the solid ground beneath his feet.

ON CALVARY HILL

1.

I may have known
when I was young
in the way an egg knows
boiling
but I did not know in the way
people say "this happened to me."

Of course I knew
about my teenage confessional
interrogations—
of touching myself impurely,
Father Matt required the details.
Agonizing out the answers
felt like part of penance.
Relieved the gender of my fantasies
bore no investigation, my young
and Catholic mind was quick to rule
all evidence inadmissible—
I concluded I was in a phase,
and he was calibrating
the dosage of my Hail Marys.

2.

I knew better about his questions
only decades later
when the court mandated
the release of documents, revealing

Numerous allegations:
  Wine and whiskey to minors
    at 13, or 14
  grabbed genitals   *—Father Matthew denies*
        the rectory
  unbuttoned pants
    the drive-in theater
      mutual masturbation
  exposed   *—Father Matthew denies*
    spiked lemonade
  16
    anal penetration
      a hotel room   *—Father Matthew emphatically denies*

The Diocesan Review Board
at the outset noted
how it is difficult
to make findings
from more than 20 years ago,
but from the totality
of the facts presented,
did determine:

it more likely than not;

thus, he was not allowed
    to exercise priestly ministry,
    to celebrate the Mass publicly,
    to administer the sacraments,
    to present himself as a priest.

He never came before a jury, no sentence
ever given, instead, the Church told him
to lead a life of prayer and penance.

3.

When the scandal first broke
I was miles and years away
from home and Church.
I simply read and listened, felt
no need to inquire, until
a visit home, mom and me alone,
she was telling stories, talking fast,
as if to outrun the stroke that soon
would steal her tongue. Father Matt
had called one day, concerned—
he said I seemed too soft, not boy
enough for him. She did not tell me
of her response, and stunned,
I did not ask. My mom was not one
intimidated by priestly office, thus,
I know her retort was razor-edged,
a restraining order served.

4.

Father Matthew made a statement
to the Review Board:
My heart goes out
to anyone who has been victimized.
I do believe
that I too am a victim.
Then he quoted Jesus:
Do you want to be my disciple?
then you must take up your cross
and follow in my footsteps.
He concluded with this prayer:
Please Lord,
give me the strength to make it up
Calvary Hill.

5.

My back is squarely turned on all
that is the Church, though I know
I'll always be a Catholic boy.
Lesson plans of shame, easy learning
for a boy like me, sentenced to mistrust
my own skin; *Oh Lord, I am not worthy,*
memorized for life. Despite years
of loving men and mending tears,
I am still doing time on that grave hill.
I try to help the boys turned men
re-learn the use of stigmata-scarred
hands and feet, but mostly I walk
among the trees, careful to avoid
the blood-stained nails scattered
on the sacred ground. Among the many
here, I've never seen a Father Matt.

NOTE: Parts 2 and 4 are found poems from documents concerning a Catholic Diocese's investigations of abusive priests, selected and re-arranged material from source documents appear in italics. The name used is a pseudonym. See the larger set of documents at: www.commercialappeal.com/church-secrets-records/letters-by-victims/.

NOTHING BUT A COW TO HELP ME FIGURE OUT WHO I AM

On a winding road, two boys
go past the Memphis city limits.
I'm behind the wheel, Mother's
station wagon, '71, burnt red,
wood-faked vinyl, on the pseudo-
leather front bench seat, Chris sits
next to me, we're absorbed.

Summer words sling
around the hot night air
that careens fast between
our open windows; we lament
our dads' boring jobs, compare
our journal keeping habits, ask
what prayer really is.

I'm cautious
on the narrow road
wondering
if Chris feels
our words like I do—
the in and out,
the mouth and ear,
the his and mine

then a cow appears,
its midnight backside
fills the road, I can't be sure,
but I think its tail sways
with the rhythm of its trot.

Oh shit, I say,

more thrill than fear,
and foot to brake, we slow,
fall in line behind the cow.
I'm now talking fast:
out of nowhere . . .
can't believe . . .
we almost . . .
I look at Chris, he says,
we gotta turn back soon.

EVAN

After gym one Fall day at Four Rivers High, my skin adolescent damp, I reach in my locker for my shirt. Glancing down I see the soft, over-washed blue of your jeans held loosely on your narrow hips. You repose against lower locker doors, your arms peppered in fine fig-brown hair, embracing your lean shirtless chest above those ribs. You look up at me, a lost boy softness in your slightly freckled face.

I catch scent of a sweat-under-soap-clean smell. My eyes widen, and my mouth fills with the taste of fruit, ripened suddenly on the tree of self-knowledge. My sophomore manliness emboldened by your freshman innocence, I slide down so naked shoulders touch, scraping my back on the bark of locker vents. I am cast out of an old place of simple order, as I say hello to you and this new life.

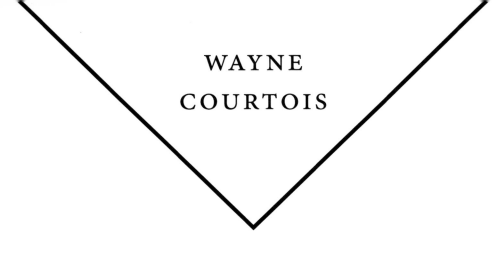

WAYNE COURTOIS

FEEL THE ETERNAL

WAYNE COURTOIS was born in Portland, Maine, and currently lives in Kansas City, Missouri, with his husband, Ralph Seligman. In January 2014 they celebrated 25 years together. A graduate of the MFA Program at the University of North Carolina-Greensboro, Wayne is author of the memoir *A Report from Winter* as well as the novels *My Name Is Rand*, *Tales My Body Told Me*, and *In the Time of Solution 9*, all published by Lethe Press. Employed as a grants manager, Wayne earned his Grant Professional Certification (GPC) in 2010 and serves on the board of the local chapter of the Grant Professionals Association. He also serves on the board of The Writers Place, a Kansas City literary community center that offers readings, workshops, panel discussions, book signings, and educational programs for all ages.

Q: What is the responsibility of the poet to the gay community?

As long as people are being tortured and killed for being gay, we need to show what's universal about the gay experience.

Q: Who are your poetry heroes?

Galway Kinnell, first, last, and always. I still have The Book of Nightmares *I bought as a college freshman in 1972. Next to Kinnell, Adrienne Rich.*

STAGES

I.

Here I am, first time hauling in air.
Oh, it's bright! Too much light!
And what are those strange creatures over there?

II.

A fat kid, always apart somehow or other.
Lonelier than a cloud on Wordsworth's day off.
Can't even make friends with my brother.

III.

Adulthood! How'd it happen?
Last I knew, I had a roof over my head.
Now I wander, shoeless, the length of Manhattan.

IV.

Maturity! Gone my shoeless days, which I just invented.
Don't matter if I never cause a ripple,
or be known for owning great things. (I only rented.)

V.

The end. And here I go, bringing to death
not much more than what I brought to life,
arriving naked and out of breath.

SOUTHMORELAND NIGHTS

A scream, a tenant mugged
beneath our bedroom window.
Maintenance guy shook his head
at the blood: "He whomped her good."

Footsteps in the parking lot
near the tiny swimming pool.
Running steps. A gunshot.
We dove for the lounge chairs.

New Year's Eve, and the old custom
of firing a gun at midnight.
Neighbors came out on their porches, again and again.
Why fire one gun when you've got several?

They weren't long, those Southmoreland nights,
and there would never be enough of them.
We held each other, too tired to speak,
our hands miming the words:

Baby, are you all right?
Are you all right, Baby?
It'll be all right, I promise.

A FEW BEAUTIFUL MOMENTS BEFORE I DIE

Don't talk to me of Cupid's fields.
I've gamboled there, in flats and heels.
Need and greed? I've been there, too,
As much as you, and you, and you.

Budged, nudged, spun, and swung,
Tapped, rapped, slightly stung,
Strapped, slapped, sapped, and sated,
Oil changed and tires rotated.

Giving up north and south poles
To the kinds of glory found in holes.
It's amazing that I've lasted.
Holy days passed, I never fasted.

But more than that—oh, so much more—
I want the one man I adore
To hold me absolutely still
While moonlight waxes on the sill.

This is why we name the seas,
The planets, stars, and galaxies,
And all the things beneath the sky.
This is why, this is why.

SATURDAY MORNING

Watering plants
on our tiny patio,
how like an angel you look
in sweatpants and T-shirt,
your thinning hair glowing.

Today we woke up, I felt
the back of your head,
hair flattened by sleep,
ears fleshy and warm.

One kiss. Another.
How can they taste
the same, always,
as if we don't change?

A tender home we have,
none too clean,
full of books and papers,
two cats denied nothing.

I see you bending
over their heads,
I see the things you love
and I love them.

And I wonder,
in those moments
when darkness
seizes me by the throat:

How do I know you won't die
and leave me alone?
How do I know you won't go,
your body turned to ashes
as you wanted?

Nothing left of you
means nothing left of me.
How, how could you,
how could you do that?

Sometimes
your smile is sad,
as if you, too, wonder
if love survives loss.

I see you watering plants,
bending over the small green shoots.
I see the things you love
and I love you.

This morning, again,
I shoulder my pain
like a knapsack
you will never see into.

I step out
onto the patio.
"Good morning, my love."
And love endures.

AD ASTRA
A Wedding Poem

I reach for you
with arms of memory,
days and nights

slipping down
my fingertips.
I close my eyes,

feel the rain
that soaked us,
sun that baked us

on the coasts of Mexico.
The snowstorm in Maine
we drove through one night:

"Don't worry," I said.
"Visibility's fine."
I couldn't see a goddamn thing.

I reach for you
on the streets of New York,
the tundra near Estes Park,

The New Orleans guesthouse
where the bedsprings rang
like sleigh bells.

The room in Key West
where we ate key lime pie in bed
like naughty boys.

The Kansas prairie
where we drove, lost, one summer night,
a miracle of stars above us.

I reach for you
in restless airports,
waiting rooms, funeral homes.

We got through the losses:
your parents, my mother and aunt,
as hard as we'd feared.

Meanwhile, picketers
and pundits likened us
to animals and pedophiles.

Two friends beaten
and left for dead,
one lost an eye, the other

his hearing in one ear.
Yes, they say we will suffer,
they say we are damned.

I see the first morning
I woke in your bed,
you in the doorway

blowing through a plastic wand,
filling the air with bubbles,
each bearing a slippery rainbow.

We are the moments
that draw us close, like
the songs and poems,

plays and movies
where we glimpse ourselves
and our hearts grow quiet.

Eternity is what it is,
the great divide.
Yet I reach for you,

and take your hand,
and feel the eternal
in us.

OURS IS NOT A DARK STORY

We should have bought a house all on one level.
No stairways. No pitfalls. No cheap walls
You can punch holes in with a paper clip.

Carpets bunch up as if the floors are shrinking.
Floors creak like the bones of the dead.
Patio wall moldy as a long-forgotten petri dish.

College student neighbors with their mess,
Garbage overflowing the curb, beer bottles
In the grass, pizza boxes like stepping stones.

I see it now, everything on one level,
No threat of a mishap, tumbling in the night.
Like so much else, it could have been.

And yet, ours is not a dark story.
When those walls start closing in,
Suffocating, annihilating,

We can punch ourselves free with a paper clip.
And those college kids, they're young and strong.
They can carry us out when it's time.

THE LOOSENING SKY

When it's too much,
the prayers and struggles,
testaments to loss,

misplaced raiments,
a stopped cross—
and *what happened when*

is as heavy
as *what might have been*,
memory's cloak

catching on pebbles
of happiness, stones
of ill fortune,

fucking cinder blocks
of disaster—forget it.
See yourself another day,

your place swept clean,
nothing astray. You're neat, too,
skin stretched over bone.

What now, in your world
of order? Did you think
you were done?

Too late, you learn
the consequence
of dropped weight:

the slipping gravity,
loosening sky.
Kiss whatever goodbye,

unhold tight.
Deep breath.
Hope you're right.

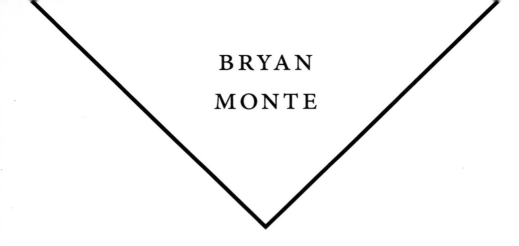

BRYAN MONTE

IF YOU EVER READ THIS

BRYAN MONTE is *Amsterdam Quarterly*'s publisher and editor. He has a BA from the University of California, Berkeley and an MA from the Brown University Graduate Writing Program. He has worked as a reporter, college lecturer, and writing instructor. His articles, essays, and reviews have appeared in the *Maui News, Poetry Flash, San Francisco Sentinel, John Whitmer Historical Association Journal*, the 1986 Doubleday anthology, *Gay Life*, and on KPFA-FM. His poetry has appeared in *Bay Windows, Friends Journal, Irreantum, The James White Review*, and *Sunstone* and in the anthology, *Gathered: Contemporary Quaker Poets*.

Q: What is the responsibility of the poet to the gay community?

The poet should be a prophet and a historian with the vision and insight to predict and chronicle what will happen and why it happened.

Q: Talk to your fifteen-year-old self. What would the poet you've become tell the boy you were?

Trust yourself, your vision, and your craftsmanship. Read the work of other poets, both living and dead. Share your good poems with the world.

WHY I LIKE THE BALLET

There was too much shouting at home
for me ever to enjoy the opera
nor is it easy for me to imagine
two dumpy, middle-aged leads
as Tristan and Isolde.
The Concertgebouw's tight seating
makes my legs burn
even before the intermission.
Besides there's nothing to look at
except the conductor
chopping and caressing thin air,
the hall's 16-foot, gold organ pipes,
as big as God's teeth, or the occasional
violin bow going the wrong direction.

No, the Dutch National ballet for me!
Its bulimic ballerinas starved to silhouettes,
just heads and hips on which to hang
tiaras and tutus twinkling
with rhinestones and sequins
shimmering in the blue-white spotlight
leaving phosphorescent wakes,
make me forget what they have to do
to get their feet into those toe shoes.

And the muscled, male principals
like Matthew Golding (What a name!)
one of the troupe's many imports
whose leaps and lifts alone
are worth twice the price of admission.
(Though you'd never have recognized him
at warm ups an hour earlier

in baggy sweats, ashen-faced, matted hair)
as he now leaps out onto stage
in his white and gold-roped
marching band top, suddenly tanned.
(They really can work miracles in Makeup).
God's drum major or a leaping lion tamer
his unruly mane now golden and under control
his white tights showing off his bulging buttocks
as hard as a horse's hindquarters.
He smiles, then lifts and twirls
yet another ballerina
without grunting or missing a step
his primal, nearly naked photo
on the program cover
feet flexed like fists
both legs bent under him in midair
a "Don't try this at home, folks"
porn star stunt showing
he's definitely won his Rite to Spring.
The real reason I go to the ballet
feeling a little lighter for two hours
before my feet stutter again across
the Stopera's brightly-lit lobby
on another rainy, windy afternoon
leaning into my cane.

THE MIRROR OF THE MEDUSA

My personality is infectious
so people keep their distance
or cover their mouths when I open mine.
An alien shipwrecked on this hostile planet
with supernatural powers x-ray and infrared
men freeze in the headlights of my glance
as I telekinetically unzip their pants.

No longer the hunted, but the hunter
mothers sweep up children in my path
warned by the beacon of my earring
I am everything everyone is talking about and more —
I am learning to conjugate their secret desires.
Say want, *wonder*, w a n d e r, WAIT!
I melt wedding bands with a single stare
I am the mirror of the Medusa.

THE PREDATORS

A view of town looking down through the night air

a shimmering bowl of heat and dust

        an undersea world

                of skyscraper stalagmites.

Men come to this rim

          to feed out of the light

      drawn by what is distant and what is present

they surface at the nexus of hills and sky

         their mouths moving fishlike

drawing in a different oxygen.

A car with out-of-state plates

        weaves awkwardly through unfamiliar hills

its chrome grill skimming the highway

        for a man a little too thin

          outside the shell of his car.

This strange food chain that tears the flesh

                                              but will not swallow

                                  that stabs his chest

                                      but leaves his wallet

his body taken up in a sudden rapture of hands

                                        and dumped in a distant river

his car left behind in the parking lot
                                              the next morning

a mute witness.

LOCO(MOTION)

It's his big hands I notice
this Friday evening
hovering before my eyes
as I sit in the jump seat
of the always crowded N-Judah
as it lurches down to Ocean Beach,
his nails' pink half moons
the orange freckles and wiry hair
just above the knuckles
and the gold band on his left hand
holding *The Chronicle* Sports Section.

His tall, lanky body bows and sways
with the rustle of Chinese vegetables in plastic bags
cymbals that leak out of headsets
and the sudden screech of the circular floor
spinning beneath him as he loses his footing
then the scratchy, spice, citrus sweat
of his woolen crotch pressed against my face.
He pushes himself away with a gasp
mumbles, *Excuse me*, his ears and neck flushed
as he reaches down to pick up his newspaper
tented and splayed around his wingtips.
It is the most anyone has touched me today,
the most anyone will touch me tonight.

THE SAX PLAYER

Thin limbed
the L of his jaw
against puffed out cheeks
dimpling
the harder he blows.
A golden J
an arm of sound
from his mouth
to his cock
hands distant
face blue-white
as if he were
about to pass out
biting the thin
silver mouthpiece.
High notes
squeal back
through the reverb
sweat drips
off his head
like a kid in a sprinkler
jumping.

KAMIKAZE

In your studio, my head is always reeling
from your kiss, the wintergreen turpentine
the plastic flowers hung from the ceiling
stolen from the dead to please the living.

Power tools and screws, fresh paint on every chair
nowhere to sit amongst the plane crash clippings
telephone receivers, hung from the ceiling, dangle in midair
to connect you with the suffering everywhere.

The doors to your bedroom are all painted black
and stenciled with the white warnings
of young pilots who never made it back
fighters diving over your bed in perpetual attack.

BILL

Think of him as another temporary worker
one of thousands in a city of millions
unsure of his next assignment
his pay changing with the nature of the work
his skills and desirability.

At 11 PM he's a sentry
standing in front of a store
hands shoved in his pockets
like pistols
eyes riveting with the precision
of a border guard checking passports
his Quaaluded veins pulse like a distant river
no emotion can cross
his blow-dried hair combed strategically over
a fresh cut on his forehead.

And at 1 AM he's a dancer
bouncing up and down on the pavement
in front of the bar
the cold radiating up through his tennis shoes
wearing a tank top in 50 degree weather.
He wants to go somewhere warm for an hour
too dangerous to stay the night.
A station wagon pulls up to the curb
the bumpers too rusted for the vice squad
the passenger door opens
the young man jumps in
and the car turns quickly
                              around the corner
                      out of the streetlights
into the night.

TO HARRY
IN THE HOPE OF YOUR SPEEDY RETURN

I do not know which city you have traveled to tonight
or which hotel room bed holds you between its sheets
like a business letter slid into an envelope

But cards sent to mark your departure
sit like phantom songsters in my mailbox
whispering at my neck and ears like cologne
against the dirty tread of faces and voices on the subway
that smudge the (memory) slight weight(lessness) of
your arm around my shoulder.

The postmarks read: Montreal   Boston
              Albany   NY
        Philadelphia   NJ
A map of the places you no longer are
your handwriting as if at sea
or on a commuter train
the "h's" falling back on themselves
the "t's" crossed lower and lower.

And I sleep in a tangle of sheets
running through a land of too much sun and sky
the ground disappearing beneath my feet
as I become weightless
not sprouting wings or fins
to swim through these deep skies
but floating higher past the clouds
suffocating in the thinning air.

AT ARM'S LENGTH

We woke every Saturday to her ringing
your mother a click in my ear
when I got to the phone first
forgetting it would be her
your father, every holiday
a white Delta 88
honking at the curb
your steps echoing
down the wooden stairs
the front door banging
and the next morning
a plate of leftovers
in the refrigerator.

Until the holiday you did not go
and I carried a Christmas tree
three miles down Hope Street
to that great, green house on West Avenue
and our dark, wood paneled apartment
decorated with the landlord's
supermarket van Gogh reproductions
your Marilyn Monroe color Xeroxes
and my posters from San Francisco and Berlin
as we huddled indoors for the next five months
from the cold rains and heavy snows
our pantry, linen closets and cupboards
stocked not with canned goods and warm clothes
but with rare gay books, tapes and records.

That Christmas we gave each other
English chocolate toffees
a blue iridescent, Italian silk sweater

the Talking Head's *Little Creatures'*
"Road to Nowhere"
and a miniature red basket
of Guatemalan worry dolls
six straw, matchstick figures
wrapped in colored thread
to carry my troubles on the 26-hour,
overnight train ride to Chicago
for my presentation at the English convention
on the suppression of the "homosexual discourse"
or "gay gaze" in Fassbinder's *Berlin Alexanderplatz*
which all my professors missed, though
I noticed the phrase in their papers years later.

The day before I left
we held the camera at arm's length
no one else to take our picture,
one of us always a little too close
missing an arm, a leg or an ear
and slightly out of focus.

The next autumn we hid
in the walk-in closet
from a hurricane that made landfall
our windows taped with white X's
so they would not shatter and cut
the secret of our love that grew and died
and no one cared
        or no one knew
                or turned away
                      or turned to stare
Medusan, like the faculty wives
their hair piled high in suspicious warning
or snickered like the bag boys
when we picked up our groceries
to walk back through the snow

the milk freezing in the cartons
before we made it home.
Two poor fags they thought
and they were right
surprised that having won the fight
we could not stay together.
Lost to each other in the same three rooms
lost to the television and the telephone
lost to the 3 AM bathroom smoking jags
or all-nighters typing in the kitchen
lost to our teeth grinding jobs
at the phone company, at high school
soothing customers' angry complaints
or students'/teachers' whispered threats
and, when I moved up North to teach,
lost to the frequent, Friday evening blizzards'
sudden and unarguable logic
the roads impassible for days
a telephone call, our only link.

You answer the phone
I ask if you are there
not recognizing your voice
after all these years
too proud to call your name again
before you say, *One moment please,*
set the receiver on the table next to the television
the chimes of a game show in the background
your topsiders sticking to the linoleum floor
as you walk across the kitchen
to run some water in the sink
before you come back and hang up
the connection crackling back to a dial tone.

If you ever read this
in the College Hill bookstore
please remember me as I do you:
the young playwright with curly, brown hair
leaning against a wooden counter
wearing a white T-shirt and green cotton pants
stroking your copper-colored beard.
The man who made me a wood scrap birthday book
inlaid with gold and silver cigarette foil
for the sun and the moon
my name inscribed inside a star
traced with whiteout on black paper
that still holds the covers together
more than a quarter century later
in the bookcase next to my desk.
The tanned, olive-skinned man
who swam naked at Moonstone Beach
while I sat in a folding chair
correcting summer school papers
writing an essay, "Living With a Lover,"
watching your strong, browned body
with its satyr's patch of black hair
in the small of your back
slip between the Atlantic's
endless blue-green scrolls
and bid me come in.

ANTHONY MOLL

GODDAMN VAN GOGH SKY

ANTHONY MOLL is a Californian expatriate living in Baltimore. He runs *Industry Night*, an online literary journal exploring the theme of work, and he is a regular contributor to Baltimore's *Gay Life* magazine. Anthony's work has also recently appeared in *Wilde Magazine*, *Seltzer Zine*, and *Gertrude*. He escaped both military service and the D.C. non-profit scene to complete an MFA with the University of Baltimore, where he now teaches.

Q: What has poetry taught you?

Poetry has taught me, and continually reminds me, how to ache in public and that it is all right to do so.

Q: Who, writing today, excites you?

Saeed Jones and Dorthea Lasky: both write words that make me want to burst.

MEMENTO

Remember when we learned to fight? I ask
when we were taught to be a war, to hump
the weight upon our backs, to charge, to shoot
the men who looked unlike our kin, to beat
our chests, to be a plague
Do you recall instead the summer sweat?
The South in May which dripped with sex
upon the floors of G.I. rooms at night
The taboo flesh of Spartan men who sparked
the thought of you and I
Bronzi di Riace, but posed anew
a sugar-burned sculpture against a wall
our trigger fingers kneading brazen flesh
we derelict enlisted men who chose
instead to be a dance

YELLOW RIBBON

Around her hair
she wore a yellow ribbon

> Remember when we learned to march?
> Learned to cherish
> the sound of our soles
>   striking asphalt
> Learned to love that ol' left
>   right left

She wore it in the springtime
and the merry month of May

> The boys of Alpha Company sleeping with
> boots lined under bunks
> bare pairs of feet
> facing and kissing
>   in the dark

And if you ask
her why the heck she wore it

> Pale blue payphones phoning home
> in fields of southern springtime
> "The weather's great;
> I can't wait to tell you
> all about it
>   love"

She wore it for the soldier
who was far, far away

ORPHEUS WITH THE AWKWARD FOOT

Twenty-four-feet tall and strumming
elegiac songs on his lyre,
the muse of the Argonauts
flexes atop a frieze of low-relief.
He is seen mid-pivot,
caught in an inelegant pose,
his back, away, but turning toward
a copse of cherry blossoms
chosen to commemorate the fallen
sentries who stood like a sea
wall before this city of monuments.
Should I miss the point instead?
Look upon this bronze Greek with lust?
This daddy of the cult of wine,
this first sodomite,
his calves contracting
his hand caught mid-stroke
his hind glowing in the spring sunlight,
the only god he chose to worship
in his winter years.

METAPOETRY: THE POETS ARE DEAD

The Poets
   (I want to fuck)
are dead.
I'm left
fantasizing:
Paris in the 1960s
        Ginsberg with hair
               Norse's mustache
               between my cheeks.

METAPOETRY: THE NEW PARISIANS

The New Parisians
drank, smoked and fucked
up verses
of American poetry
on the moon-kissed tops
of roofs
of American poets
laughing, flirting and inhaling
the goddamn van Gogh sky.

METAPOETRY: UNWASHED BODIES

Unwashed bodies
resting on pristine sheets
where they came
      to rest
Mired in sentiment
refusing to rinse
a body ripe
      with poetry

CENTO: ON WALKING

Who wishes to walk with me?
Will we stroll dreaming of the lost America of love
rolling and rolling there
where God seems not to care;
in the warm New York 4 o'clock light we are drifting back and forth
between each other like a tree breathing through its spectacles.
Look upward. Neither firm nor free
remember always walking
through halls of cloud
down aisles of sunlight,
"That cloud looks like a fish,
and that cloud looks like a fairy!"
Here is some halo
the living made together.

Credits, by line:

Whitman – "Song of Myself"
Ginsberg – "Supermarket in California"
Owen – "Greater Love"
Owen – "Greater Love"
O'Hara – "Having a Coke"
O'Hara – "Having a Coke"
Gunn – "Black Jackets"
Swenson – "Earth your Dancing Place"
Swenson – "Earth your Dancing Place"
Swenson – "Earth your Dancing Place"
Gibson – "Asking too Much"
Gibson – "Asking too Much"
Doty – "At the Gym"
Doty – "At the Gym"

MICHAEL MONTLACK

SHOW A LITTLE MORE LEG

MICHAEL MONTLACK is the author of the poetry book *Cool Limbo* (NYQ Books, 2011) and the editor of the Lambda Finalist essay anthology *My Diva: 65 Gay Men on the Women Who Inspire Them* (University of Wisconsin Press, 2009) as well as its "sister" poetry anthology *Divining Divas* (Lethe Press, 2012). He has been awarded residencies at (or scholarships from) the Virginia Center for the Creative Arts, the Ucross Foundation, Lambda Literary Retreat, and the Community of Writers at Squaw Valley. Montlack splits his time between New York City, where he teaches at Berkeley College, and the West Coast.

Q: What four people would appear on a Mount Rushmore of gay poetry?

For American-born queer poets: Gertrude Stein, Walt Whitman, Elizabeth Bishop, Allen Ginsberg.

Q: Talk to your fifteen-year-old self. What would the poet you've become tell the boy you were?

The title of a Peter Cameron novel sums up what I would say to my fifteen-year-old self: Someday This Pain Will Be Useful to You.

DICKORUM

Decorum: noun. The dignified propriety of behavior, speech, dress, etc.

Dickorum: The not-so-dignified propriety of behavior, speech, dress for (and between) SOME gay men.

Dickorum is . . . when that totally cute guy you just met at the bar (and so want to ask out to dinner) leaves suddenly with somebody else, shouting at you from across the dance floor, in front of all your friends, and your cousins from out of town, "Hey, I'll just catch ya at the sex club later, kay?"

Dickorum is realizing that no, he isn't joking.

It's not letting on that a joke even crossed your mind.

It's also you instantly considering making your first visit there. Hoping that maybe you could find the guts to ask him out, if you could actually muster the nerve to parade around and then approach him in nothing more than a too-small towel. Dickorum's also not even trying to offer those cousins of yours an explanation. For his comment. Or for your leaving them with your friends for the rest of the night—once you finally decide to do it—giving them the address for where to meet you for brunch the next day and then heading over to the sex club.

Dickorum is acting like you've been to a sex club before. So the door guy won't think you naïve. It's saying you know all the rules already and taking just the one-night membership because you "left" your yearly card at home.

It's pretending to bump into that totally cute guy (after you've stalked him for half an hour, mousing through the maze of dim hallways clogged with men posing in shadows that conceal the parts that least flatter them) and then laughing, looking surprised, muttering, "Oh my god, I SO thought you were joking about coming here. I mean, I've never seen you here before."

It's not hesitating to go back to his little room. Then apologizing for not wanting to go beyond handjobs just yet. It's persuading him that holding out means you like him, that a blowjob or fucking would mean you didn't see his potential. It's also not even blinking when he says that he'd love dinner sometime but can't. Because his boyfriend only allows meaningless fucks but nothing more. It's also not asking what he means when he mentions that it's bad enough his poor wife doesn't know about his boyfriend. Then it's fucking him anyway. To make sure he thinks you're not at all disappointed. And it's not kissing his beautiful full lips while you fuck him. It's kissing him goodbye on the cheek instead—after he's cum and you've realized that he's not interested in waiting for you to cum. "Enjoy the rest of your night," you say after he tells you to go easy on those poor boys. It's not responding when he says, "So I'll catch ya at the bar next week?" It's letting him see you enter someone else's room. Then clumsily excusing yourself from that room. Once you're sure that enough time has passed for him to have showered and left the club.

MEMORY

is the dress
that once fit
perfectly.

Loosening
or pulling with age.

Idealism and denial—
its accessories.
Which don't often match.
And regularly change
with the seasons.

GEOGRAPHIC POLYGAMY

New York:
Your wife, the one
you could never leave,
almost a little afraid of her,
sometimes smelling like her,
not being able to sleep nights
without the sound
of her snoring.

San Francisco:
Your mistress, the other love
of your life, the one you regularly leave,
knowing it's just better this way,
this fantasy too bright, too
curvy, just too whimsical
to really believe you
could keep her
to yourself.

Portland (Oregon):
The fuck buddy you bike with
up the coast occasional summers,
berry picking naked by day
and bear-hugging nights
in the tent—even
when it's not
that cold.

Barcelona:
That week-long affair
you had backpacking Europe—
its harmony no doubt

resting on your
language
barrier.

Long Island:
The girl next door
you were supposed to
marry but just couldn't,
knowing she would never
leave. While you—you
already had your
bags packed.

DISCO *INFERNO*

In the Seventh Circle,
the sodomites ran,
aimed into their own
direction
      against traffic
on the fiery sands,
licking blisters
across their sandal-less soles
—the brimstone fueling
leaden lungs
and clouding the view
of no finish line.

*

In the seventh month,
the boys ferry,
aimed for their own
beaches,
      avoiding traffic
on the Fire Island sands,
sunscreening tans
with rich moisturizing salves
—tea dance fog machines
misting pecs,
blurring the edge
of parties with no end.

DICKORUM

Is your boss emailing (after seeing your profile for the first time on Manhunt one night) to ask if you finished that budget analysis for him yet . . . before he compliments your cockshot. In a parenthesized PS.

Dickorum is answering him. "Sorry, I'll need another day or two on that. And thanks. I like your fisting pics. Seems your hubby's very talented."

Dickorum's also immediately realizing (after you hit send) that maybe that isn't his hubby (Oh my god, it's Bob from Accounting!) but not correcting yourself, just letting it go.

Finally, Dickorum is not even blushing as you pass his cubicle the next morning. No wink from him. No smile. Nothing. Just a "how'd you make out?" that you almost answer before realizing he doesn't mean the budget figures. It was a greeting, a coded good morning. So just keep walking. And sure—you can take an extended gander at Bob if you want, but not long enough to suggest you're interested. Unless of course you're into fisting.

Because Dickorum says don't cock tease. Or ass tease. Or put up your "dukes" . . . unless you mean it.

A HIGH WAY TO HELL
AFTER CHIP LIVINGSTON'S "THE FAVORABLE WITNESS"

Truckstop: public turnstyle club

for spies of the tight smiles,

a homesick sucker's release circuit.

Shaken bottles of mood mounting:

white rush into the porcelain flush.

A remembering of animals, cuts, throats,

awkward belongings, somehow comfortable

fever. Yesterday's crumpled route

to recovered indulgence? "Don't spit!"

Your devotionless devotion. Denim-ed

undoings. And then, "Please, Sir. Some more?"

When too many was not enough. "Get!"

A grip on a hairy ankle: a sailorboy's only anchor.

Fluid expressway: snake of yellow lights.

"Boy, where do ya think you're going?"

Slithering toward exhaustion. Watch now.

"Yeah, watch." See how often it never comes.

MEDUSA—JUST ANOTHER RUSH LIMBAUGH "SLUT"?

That's how he'd see it, saying she had
no right to be there in the first place.
Somewhere as serious as Athena's temple.
Saying *She obviously didn't know her place.*
Like that Sandra Fluke marching into Congress!
Only a lawless prostitute could be so bold . . .
bowing at the altar of a female God?
Come on, people—what next? Flying horses?
And maybe if she hadn't been so darn pretty—
no doubt gussying herself up
for chance meetings with the male Gods—
she wouldn't have tempted poor Poseidon
going about his godly unslutty business.
She can cry *Rape!* all she wants
but Rush would need to see the video tapes
before making any judgments.
I mean, had she just stayed home
balancing olives between her knees,
instead of hitting the Pagan orgy circuit,
there wouldn't have been any trouble.
Or need for contraception. Or punishment.
She wouldn't have been made into
so ugly, so evil, so useless a woman
that even her parents would be ashamed.
As ugly as only a slut could be.
Ugly enough to actually kill a man.
Bring him down without even having to strike.
          Only in his own mirror would he see her ugliness.
And live to talk (radio) about it.
But even then the description he'd share
would be just too ugly to believe.
Too unbearable for anyone
to continue listening.

130   ASSARACUS

MODERN ALPHABETICAL DISORDER

What do we know

about atoms & Adam
apples & blossoms
the bees/the birds   cages
concentration camps Death-
defying & denying Duty
Empires: England, Egypt, etc . . .
Freedom, flight/fight: filibuster garbage
governmental gangs hacking
H-bomb heaven
internal-Independence
imaginary imitation junk
jingles jailing kindergarteners
khaki Kryptonite laws
liquidating legitimate
martini-migraine matters never-
never-land neutrality
New-Testament overdose
on Oedipus oil-patriarchy
penis-perjury protecting
quote: "quantity vs. quality" Renaissance
re-issuing Republican
Saint sanctuary self-tributes
terror-to-territory treaties
threatening
ulterior Utopia unravel, vacuumed
vacillating
Vogue Wild-
western wisdom X-rated
Xeroxed xenophobic
Yankee Yuppie yoyos
zigzagging this Zeitgeist
zeroed zoo?

MICHAEL MONTLACK

THAT'S "MS. PRIDE" TO YOU

As thin as you are,
almost papery—a ragged flag
wisping about in the breeze
created by the floats
and the marchers themselves,
I spotted you
waving stiffly yet regally:
Hostess to a nearly empty bus.

A powdered, bent stick
in a forest of muscular trunks and glittery foliage—
your sagging arms and spotted hands inspire
the pretty boys behind the barricades
to make an extra trip to the gym this week,
spread the sunscreen on a little thicker.

Give it up, honey!
There's a run in those hose—
No, wait! WAIT!
It's just a run in his skin.

You beam at them and show a little more leg.
Like an old aunt grateful to have family at the holidays,
you hear only youth in the cruelty.
You straighten your sash.
Boys will be boys, you might say
if there were another Stonewaller beside you,
if they hadn't all died.
Or better yet—*Boys will be girls*.

You're not even the ghost
of a beauty queen veiled by time

or your five o'clock shadow.
But as you sweat, beaded
like your brocade pumps
in this late June heat
on this narrow, packed Village street—
the satin back of your gown
speckled like a worker's flannel—
I see a teacher on that yellow bus,
a lesson for all
in your lifted skirt.

DICKORUM

Dickorum says you can sleep with your friend's ex-boyfriend after a reasonable amount of time . . . Dickorum says a reasonable amount of time can be calculated by dividing his ex's hotness by how close you and your friend truly are. Then multiplying that by the likelihood of your friend sleeping with one of your own ex-boyfriends.

If that math is too hard, just wait for a full month after their break-up. Or two to three weeks and call it a month. Close enough. If your friend freaks out, just say you thought he was totally over that loser, that you are surprised he'd even care. If your friend persists . . . say you did it to get back at him for sleeping with YOUR ex. When he denies it, which after all is likely since you made all that stuff up, just point out that at least you aren't denying what you did. That you were only trying to level the playing field. So you could go back to being the close friends you once were.

Dickorum also says don't worry if your friend doesn't buy all this. He'll totally get over it once he finds a new boyfriend. Especially if the new one is hotter than his ex.

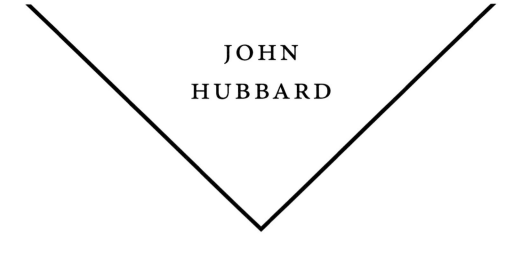

JOHN HUBBARD

Loose Leaves

JOHN HUBBARD was born in London in 1957 but has spent nearly all of his life in the English southern coastal counties of Hampshire and Dorset, where he was educated and has taught English and English Literature for many years to people from the ages of 11 to 85. He loves the home he's shared with his partner David for the last twenty-seven years, ten minutes from the beach, and enjoys maintaining the garden. He is currently working on a group of poems about life within the home called Domestic Sphere. He has had poems published in *South*, *Inclement*, and *Stimulus:respond* in the last couple of years, has been long-listed for the Bridport Prize, and was a winner of the East Anglia Poetry Competition at the King's Lynn Festival as long ago as 1980.

Q: What are you currently reading, and what have you learned from it?

The Richard Burton Diaries: *be very careful with booze; reading is a greater pleasure than money.*

Q: Who are your poet heroes?

Thomas Hardy, C.P. Cavafy, Elizabeth Bishop, Philip Larkin, Carol Ann Duffy.

BOAT

The till rang in a seaside shop,
a tangy cave where wood
and plastic mingled with salt air:
spades, buckets, balls,
pale bats, stumps and bails,
splint-mounted paper flags,
windmills and starfish moulds.
But the boat was his.

The craft satisfied his hold:
square red hull, white deck
(the brittle derricks and hooks
destined never to lift a load)
a solid bridge and superstructure
where he snapped on the blue funnel
with a lad's clumsy fingers.

One dull day, wet string unknotted,
the vessel lapped gently beyond his reach,
diminishing in the tide's subtle pull,
to melt in tears and distance.
Here clouds broke lemon white
and, in perfect profile,
a big, real boat steamed southwards;
the infinite promise of a curved world,
not quite held by rust, plunge and chain.

PROFESSOR Z____ ABROAD

WHY SHOULD THE AGED EAGLE STRETCH ITS WINGS?

T. S. ELIOT "ASH WEDNESDAY"

… Eugenides,
He organised my lowland travels,
The Smyrna merchant, in the days I went
Largely to El Iskandria, Beyrouth, Amman.
But he's long gone. Now I head west,
Where I pass unnoticed with greater ease,
Though the years have helped; nigh on two thousand,
Since I was given a reverent glance. Knees
Bend these days to damaged flesh, godhead dying.
But my desire is life and now, older
Travelling alone I love youth the more.

From the south, where hawks wheel above woods' shades,
Turning fields of yellow heads, bearded maize,
I came swift to Paris, amused myself
With Louvre drawings of my cup-bearer:
Always a little plump, the face too plain.
In a number I looked fine, full-feathered—
But for such boys I'd not have stretched a wing.
Yet before Flandrin's oil of the nude lad
I felt toe nails itch to talons, down plume
On my chest, fade as I moved on in haste.

But on the train, reading Proust (Volume Four,
What else if you have all eternity?)
The boy walked in, an ephebe, a student,
You would say, nineteen perhaps: shorts, sweatshirt,
Red backpack, gracious with the old, their bags,
Flexuous, beautiful. My eagle eye
Swivelled, could not look away from curly hair,
Soft looks, strong chest, shoulders, legs. Auale sprang

Behind my thumbs unbidden, fingers hot
Would have sprung primaries, but for firm will.
Once I ruled a universe, now I scarce
Can rule myself. My book fell, unnoticed
As he drank the passing trees and hills with joy
As if the world were new to him. We stopped,
He paced the platform, restless a while,
Smiled straight at me. For soaring then
No air was high enough.

                  I recognised
On his luggage label an outpost where
I was worshipped under a Roman name.
I had intended to travel westward
Along the coast, tangle with rough rocks, see
My colleague P_____, the oceanographer.
My excuses scumbled in the ferry's wake,
Transparently. Over the hours the boy
Passed several times, caught my averted eye
And longing's direct force.

                  My final glimpse
Was at the port, running for his home train,
Running towards his life, and at his heels
I saw bright wings, knew I had put them there.

In the hotel bathroom I bathed my feet,
Snacked—toast and honey—went to bed alone,
Dreamt of flying.

What can one offer mortals when dethroned?

RUE DU MARAIS, BRUXELLES, 1966

This flat will never lose the smell
of her mother's bulky, camphorated furs,
which she is filling with age and girth.
Traces of her youth still snag, surprise
like looped threads of fine lace
hiding heavy mahogany,
hanging behind velvet at high windows,
catching at rings.

The bruised shine of a showery day
falls on the single over-mantel photograph:
a strong face above a uniform collar,
studio serious, still twenty-three;
the glass and silver polished and dusted
to quell the damage of fifty years.

This October she had driven to the fields
where it was thought he lay, noted
the sugar-beet piled like earthy ordnance,
wondered what goodness from him plumped their pith,
finding use, the surface once more,
atoms easing in the slant of sun.

She did not notice the lorry, fully loaded
turning from the refinery gates
or consider the sifted crystal whiteness
heading for the chocolatier.

After weekly confession at Notre Dame,
while taking coffee in the sloping square,
she tries not to look at her box from Wittamer's,
nodding its ribbons at the white cloth.

Later, she does not suspect how close to him she comes,
among her cushions, listening to her wireless,
the fire settling in the grate, lifting sweet after sweet
to lips that he had kissed long before.

MONSIEUR PAUL
VERLAINE AT ST. ALOYSIUS SCHOOL, BOURNEMOUTH, 1875

Softly pale, a voice imbued
With remnants of a solitude,
Employed, he leaves my father's door.

Our native speaker for a year,
Accenting voices bright and clear,
For which the parents could pay more.

* * *

He's walking in the shaded Chine
A special strolling place of mine,
Where heath meets cliff and shore.

He stands, attentive to the dance
Of waves receding south to France;
Tide pulls his body's core.

My own mind caught, to tell the truth,
By gestures to the swimming youth
I can't meet as before.

* * *

The month's end brings no mysteries;
He keeps in check each class with ease,
His trick a smiling roar.

He makes them play with phrase and rhymes
So well that there are many times
They feel their own tongue poor.

Old Spate, quite shaken by the noise
Of fifteen happy learning boys,
Demands I visit and deplore.

Father, well used to such requests,
Concedes, unsmiling, yet suggests
Our seniors on the upper floor.

* * *

'Prénoms, en Français,' —a surprise.
Timms, 'Arthur,' perfectly replies;
A glimmer brims his master's eyes.

LIME TREES
FOR STC

June, and locked in beneath
his bright green bell-jar:
silly old Sam of the scalded foot
in fact neglects the confines
of his prison, and roams in mind
as easily down dell and up hill,
in sight of sea and sail
as his lamented friends.

A patient week's remand would bring
pale stars opening in hundreds,
serrated shells hatching
the sweetest drifts of scent,
sprinkling his clothes
with powders and with gentle bees.

After the sentence of a month
those unmated buds would dry,
falling at his feet in golden drifts,
dense as an Egyptian tomb
brought to new light.

But a day's grumbling custody
is not enough for this.

He should trust more to trees.

STOLEN PAINTINGS

Camille Pissarro, memories of Caracas,*1850*,
and Louveciennes, *1870*

It's what I didn't paint I miss:
the press in narrow alleys, bright cloth,
whitewashed churches obscured
by the broad hands of palms,
a sky emptied of swallows
settling on their return in an August spring,
the city air thick with the grace notes
of angry passion or seduction,
Sabbath eves' solemn quiet at home,
while outside swaying mestisas
strolled with baskets at their hips.

So much I did was composition:
a mountain's slopes mirrored by the clouds;
curved trunks, figures, rocks
at measured distance;
a black donkey's panniers
balancing the weight of a shaded bush;
workers in studied conversation,
strolling home from fields.

Let some Prussian feel, smiling at his wall,
he has laid hands on something real.

A GUN
PAUL GACHET, FILS

Father did not know I had it.
July light ran its finger down the barrel
in the dimness of the cave behind the house,
flecking the oily sacking in my hands.

Vincent loved wine from the south,
holding its colour to the sun.
Father would give him a bottle,
'Good stuff. For slow drinking.'
One more bulge for his retreating back.

'Came home bleeding and in pain,'
I caught the village boy's message.
Father gone, I sought
the empty space I knew I'd find,
felt the sickness that belongs to storms.

Since the funeral we often sit
around the orange table in the yard.
The dogs skulk and whimper as I pass.

TRIPTYCH

I. Summer Scars

Dr Simpson noticed
the whiter scattering
as the boy turned the page.

Perhaps a year ago,
some summer wave, some overbalancing,
some unsustainable daring
shook out another arc
from the line, the loop
of surf- or skateboard
or parkour distance
to hurl performance from intention
on some shingle—
spattering blood on a tanned right arm
raised inadequately
against the biting ground.

They have met three times a week for five years.
He has marked essays, exchanged brief words,
seen that perfect head turn
like a Roman figure of the baroque;
those lips puffed in anguish
at a complex question;
and annually seen him sprint
with a wild intent to win.

Today
his gravelled ignorance
grates.

II. Keys

(Re: The estate of the late Dr Kenward Simpson,
of Clarence Terrace, Stourmouth.)

Jim Foster guesses the key from the bunch,
correctly as it happens,
and sees the pull of its Yale teeth
on the morning cobweb.
A stiff door opens on the stuff of gardens,
salty odours of potting shed, the silence of terra cotta,
rusted forks and trowels hardly worth a sale.

The bachelor study is familiar:
books piled high on tables,
Shakespeare essays now never to be marked,
the five-bar gate pipe rack.
The two small zinc are for the window locks,
the long bright metal with a single tooth
and double collar, nineteenth century,
are for the rattling desk drawers.

All but one are open,
yielding cheque stubs, tax returns,
correspondence on household business,
investment and travel plans, insurance,
all meticulously in order.

There is a knack to turning
the owner would have known at once,
but the lock falls away
into the thin narrow front.
Within, the testator abroad,
imaged against sands, streets, palms,
temples, in rooms, aging over the years,
often with youth after smiling youth,

sturdy, about seventeen,
and studio portraits of prefects,
black and white, later colour,
uniformly handsome,
with the familiar grammar school tie.

The lawyer leans back
considering as usual the wisest course.
Yet this web of unsettling affections
was broken with that last breath,
flaring again only to him
as day-blue flowers on a distant vine,
tinged violet like a lighter's flame.

III. Healing

The reminder of the brightness of blood,
its translucence takes away the pain
at first, of the gouge or scrape or slice.

Cool water cleans with its transparency, yet
cannot stop that blooming from the wound,
blurring rivulets across fine creases.

Slowly it stops to leave a thin glaze
hueing over days to chestnut, deepening to crust.
Sometimes the antiseptic fails, surrounding skin

blushes in irritation, edges weep first clear
then thickly white. Imperfect scabs fall
to shower and towel and the process

starts again, little by little as the dry shores
creep to shallow union like a shrinking sea
imaged by satellite year on year.

This pale reminder stays, starred through tan
until next summer, never quite gone.

Healing is thorough, not oblivion.

DOMESTIC ARCHAEOLOGY

Having all the neglect
that only daily use can supply,
the shoe cleaning box
rattles its jumbled tins
of cracked and crusted creams.
Granulated wax blooms white
like weary chocolate.

A collection, shifted without thought
to our first house,
added to by time. This
I used on those awful shoes
I wore the first time we met.
These dusty sprays waterproofed
walking boots, two pairs ago.

Three sets of brushes—'on' and 'off'
for black, dark and light brown;
my own originals, and those that came
on the deaths of our fond fathers
who taught us about pride and shine,
their bristles interlocked in tidy pairs
shouldering the story of our male marriage.

SPECTACLES

These no longer do for reading:
what makes a pine's needles show at a distance
dizzies words to confusion.
I buy another pair
for years to come, more solid, less fashionable.

Walking into the bathroom
in the mirror I see my father
dead these twenty years
walking to greet me
in the jumper of his I still wear.
There is shock on both our faces.

THE DEAD

The dead surprise us,
not with ghosts,
but with the look
of a lakeside room in a film,
the advice recalled
at an awkward junction,
the sound of a saw's note
rising in the cut,
the thought that we must tell them this,
and the pause of absence,
tugging at our startled souls,
hoping that they know.

JACK MICHAELSON

HIGH SCHOOL

JACK MICHAELSON is a student of Catholic theology in Boston, Massachusetts, originally from Missouri. He received his BA in Public Policy, Sociology, and Theology in 2012. He has been writing poetry since discovering the medium in his undergraduate career after being diagnosed with and undergoing treatment for cancer at age 22. Jack loves his family and friends dearly, because even when they lose patience with him, it means that they had patience with him in the first place. He would imagine this to be incredibly difficult.

Q: Talk to your fifteen-year-old self. What would the poet you've become tell the boy you were?

The wrestling team is not worth anorexia. The chapters of Catch-22 *are not in chronological order. Your bleached hair is more Bart Simpson than Ivan Drago.*

Q: What poem should we read aloud right now?

Read "What I Said at Her Service" by Mary Oliver aloud in front of someone you love, alive or deceased.

A SCOUT'S SAUDADE, OR *A NINETEEN FIFTY-FOUR ROCKWELLIAN AMERICA*

I.

We must all,
        at one point or another,
give up justice for fairness,
compassion for care,
liberty for freedom,
freedom to preserve the snapshots of morality
exposed in the darkroom of our hearts.

Photos and postcards from back trails
developed boys into men in our
        Nineteen Fifty-Four Rockwellian America.

When you trust and you doubt trust,
you are loyal and you abandon loyalty,
you are brave and you fear bravery,
deceit is honesty,
lying is patriotism,
ignorance is strength.

That evangelical *W.*'s signature is engraved
        on my Eagle Scout plaque.

America's basic cable evangelists
        in *Ministry of Love*
know in their darkroom hearts I hold
        a thought-crime
        a sex-crime
against nature, against God, against them—
distort my divine image.

When words shed feathers and

assume an alien plumage,
        we pray—
things are renewed.

II.

Day breaks.
Celestial fuses blown,
        electricity crackles,
red light of doom and love burns at horizons.

Religious zeal always ablaze,
flashing swords in blinding skies
        over silver peaked horns.

Hydrogen burns orange in self-passion,
thundering, lightening, talking sheer flame
with 700 American evangelists.

Pummeled awake on the banks of Nim's Lake,
thundering white capped waves race shoreward—
        last night's storm—
in the waves' hollow
rocks and stones flung
on the mud, reeds, weeds.

The sparkle of the sea in the sky—
rotting boats, flotsam of bygone stars.

The sun proclaims final decay,
the finite mass and crushing gravity of
        the sun must fail.
But Heaven teaches it
how to bathe planets in light after entombment in shadows,
how to forge iron in blood and calcium in bone—
things are renewed.

III.

The hike begins.
Vagrant under Missouri oak and pine,
        dust caked hiking boots,
faded scout socks dinge as we follow the sun west.

The Sacred splinters through dewy translucent leaves,
fracturing the yellow sunlight cascading on our heads
        mimicking a halo,
        falling off and smashing on grit.

The American evangelical basic cable club
worries we might get too close.

Here and there green light,
not through stained glass,
but tumbling from tree branches,
relieves the horror of darkness
in thickets trying to shut out light.

The world proclaims final decay,
the exhausted hills and impoverished veins of
        the earth must fail.
But Heaven teaches it
how to clothe trees after being stripped bare,
how to color flowers and open again—
things are renewed.

IV.

Dusk descends.
Crisp blue night on Nim's Lake dock
        rocks like teenage hormones—
the iron cables keep us anchored
to limestone and granite.

The Milky Way guides sailing ships

and dung beetles alike
far from the choking smoke of incinerators.

Indigo orbs lift and scatter
along gentle ripples from sky gazers,
purple colors play.

For basic cable evangelists, perpetual thunder,
in love with lightning, clanging and jolting,
among dandelion parachutes and
friends at age sixteen,
  I'm a monster.

The darkness proclaims final decay,
the hastening isolation and heat death of
   the universe must fail.
But Heaven teaches it
how to harbor life in the cruelty of space,
how to foster love in the face of emptiness—
things are renewed.

V.

In our Nineteen Fifty-Four Rockwellian America,
when you trust and you suspect trust,
you are loyal and you betray loyalty,
you are brave and you slink from bravery,
deceit is honesty,
lying is patriotism,
ignorance is strength.

America's basic cable evangelists
  in Ministry of Love
know in their darkroom hearts I hold
  a thought-crime
  a sex-crime
against nature, against God, against them—
  distort my divine image.

In homo-genital fear, homogeneity
smelts uniform plastic army figures,
the basic cable evangelists Party,
          a lone star risen in the wilderness.

Plastic army figures can be themselves now.

When words shed feathers and
assume an alien plumage,
          we pray—
things are renewed.

Our culture proclaims final decay,
the fading warmth and hopeless spite of
          the human must fail.
But Heaven teaches it
how to bond in anonymous Northern cities,
how to extend kinship in small Southern towns—
things are renewed.

BUFU, MISSOURAH

Down in Bufu, Missourah, the seat of Cassum County,
on MO Highway 67, past Irondale, closed in '65,
past Farmington, but before Fredericktown,
if you hit Fredericktown you've gone 10 too far,
lives the wilderness.

Past Arnold, then Imperial, then Barnhart, Pevely, Festus,
take a right where it says BONNE TERRE/DESLOGE, keep going straight,
past the truck beds filled with camp gear,
down the split highway, cross the oncoming
into the woods.

Drive through nature's disco, fractal lights and wooden walls,
around the bends in Scout Tower Road, through the loop 'round HQ,
down the gravel road through the gray dust
cross the power cut where the ticks live
to your summer home.

Spend a week pulling weeds, catching snakes, moving canoes,
beat woodland paths, hose down latrines, practice campfire skits,
train the lifeguards, find the ivy,
pitch the tents up, raise the flies,
no rest for the staff.

Days are long and work is hard, but our uniforms are crisp,
muscle memory flips the neckerchief for a tight fit through the slide,
socks are straightened, smiles are bright,
this is Boy Scouts, we do things right
in front of the scouts.

Prepare the native ceremonies, acrylic face paint bought at Walmart,
applied with cotton swabs to mimic the Nusquam Tribe,
this Indian regalia is all collectors items,
this feather headdress was made by hand,
it's super authentic.

We don't swear and we don't sit, we don't grow out our beards,
our staff picture just might drive Norman Rockwell to tears,
clean cut kids, Eagle Scouts,
never untucked, never out,
not even to ourselves.

Days on lead to nights off, piling in the trucks
trekking off to the Walmart, the one in Farmington,
nights at the fire tower, off 67,
stars forever, and some cigars
take the edge off.

Shooting the shit up in the sky, watching the world burn,
civilian slacks and T-shirts, no one to impress,
have you got a girl? well what's her name?
you sure talk funny. dude, are you gay?
man, that shit ain't cool.

Signed up to teach swimming, never thought I'd have to act,
turned to smoking for the stress, made it through a whole pack,
do the side stroke, don't drown in your fear,
days on the lakefront, nights in the trees,
doesn't happen nowhere else.

Last scouts head back to the town as August starts to crown,
the moon ignites my quiet goodbye, my dad's truck all packed,
I saw the sign in the rearview mirror,
stars twinkled above its shimmer
WELCOME TO THE RANCH.

Gathered greens will always turn brown, cut pine will always parch,
when you dig up rooted verdure, you stunt the young man's heart,
once we found a pine dry like Ezekiel's bones,
lit that sucker up and watched the blaze
consume the forest night.

Down in Bufu, Missourah, the seat of Cassum County,
on MO Highway 67, past Irondale, closed in '65,
past Farmington, but before Fredericktown,
if you hit Fredericktown you've gone 10 too far,
lived the wilderness.

TAYLOR SWIFTBOAT

Gay potato orange sex caught my eye. Who was this man,
this runner, this swimmer, this scientist, who laughed at
gay potato orange sex?

That glorious August afternoon, gold flakes filtered
down in shafts through my neighbor's tree and warmed
my shirtless torso, copper from summer, toned from weights.
The ether was colored with a goldenrod crayon. The air
enveloped me with heat, billows of convection cloaked me.
I could have been naked and still protected from the
oncoming dusk. And you called to make sure I was real.

Minerva carried you south to the balmy comfort of
my backyard. I wore my white trunks to contrast my tan
and left the gate open for you to come find me. And you did.

That coy smile of a man more concerned with preventing
cavities than having bleached pearls. That dirty blond buzz
of a man more concerned with preventing bed head than
having Lambert's updo. That fair freckly skin of a man
more concerned with sun protection than sun tanning.
Those rugged calves of a man more concerned
with running that extra mile and swimming that extra lap
than keeping off that extra calorie. *In my backyard.*
It was, splendid.

A handshake cut through the humidity and our towels were tossed
on the plastic table, and we tentatively stepped into the warm waters
of self introductions and self adjustments that flow from any
encounter with another member of the family labeled in our minds as
"him?"

Gliding aside the pool vacuum and floating in this new man's mystery,
guitars tinkled from the alternative station

on the '70s 8-track player slash radio
that was banished to the backyard after the kids had grown
old enough to demand modernity.

Twilight threatened us softly from above.
Our shoulders submerged under the bath water
for warmth after the sky was ripped off
by the setting of the sun, the celestial zipper that lets
the fly down and disrobes the heavens, showing the spectacle of stars
once hidden by "atmospheric refraction" you explained.
You did say you studied engineering.

Partly exhausted from treading water,
partly from regaling ourselves with pomp,
          partly from constant retucking,
we sat on a ledge with water up to our nipples and looked up.
Sagittarius did not look down, but rather,
burned at the galactic center
among star clusters and ionized nebulae.
Want to catch a movie and get pizza?

Sausage, mushroom, and *A Beautiful Mind.*
Toweling off as the delivery man came around, triggering the
floodlights, I grabbed a diet Pepsi and got you a water, tipped the
delivery man, and welcomed you into my basement studio, where
our nipples became rock hard and our goosebumps popped up
from the air conditioning. We threw on some ribbed tanks and
sweatpants and sat with the pizza on a TV tray between us.
Russell Crowe barely got to Princeton before you asked,
Would you like to cuddle?

I was little spoon. My head was lower than yours and we each
rested them on the decorative pillows. Your right hand came and
rested on my rib, and my left hand came to become intertwined
in your fingers. Our thumbs twiddled. Then we had enough.

I rolled over to face you, and your eyes were already closed.
Your chin extended so your mouth could meet mine. A beautiful

sigh escaped you as we met, and my hand glided along the contours
of your muscle tee to your back, as you did the same, and we became
close, until the weak nuclear force pushed our electrons apart.
You took a swig of water, and I warmed your cold kisses like a sunrise.

Whenever you came home from engineering school, we met.
You loved it when I licked your neck and helped you feel.
I loved it when you looked into my eyes.
I saw us growing old together.
I saw the universe. I saw you.

The last night we were together, you rested your head on my chest
and we stared off into the drop ceiling in the dark, a vast array of
picks and pocks of black on a white sky greyed by dimness.
You know, all theology is anthropology, you said, as we talked about
you heading out west to explode atoms and poke inside, throwing
clocks at each other and sifting the rubble for cogs that could betray
the secret to time. I thought *How asinine? No shit, Sherlock?*
I said, *Well, I'm tired, I should probably head to bed,*
and I walked you to Minerva, and she carried you away.

A different August, freshly stateside, time to rehash. I confessed
to you over America's great telecommunications network
I've still had feelings for you for the past several months.
You, being the particle physicist, the smartest man I know,
I know you have, and I really, really didn't want to hurt you.
I, the dumbest man I know,
I still love you.
You,
I love you as well, but as a close friend.
I can't say I can be your lover.
It's hard for me to say that, but I know I have to.

I will not Taylor Swiftboat* you.

---

* The term *swiftboating* is an American neologism used pejoratively to describe an unfair or
untrue political attack. The term is derived from the name of the organization "Swift Boat
Veterans for Truth" because of their widely publicized then discredited campaign against 2004
US Presidential candidate John Kerry. Taylor Swift is a popular American singer-songwriter.

This is not an attempt at revenge.
I do hope the land of Sheriff Joe Arpaio
     and Jan Brewer
     and Higgs Bosons
treats you well, filled with purple sunsets
     and swimming pools
     and air conditioning
and maybe on a starry night, you could go outside in August
and look up, and maybe, see Sagittarius looking down at you,
the teapot constellation, floating in space,
with the reddit Snoo looking lovingly down at the posts under
     r/atheism**
and one of us, it doesn't matter who, will say
I'll catch you later bud.

** The mascot for r/atheism is the Reddit Snoo in a teapot floating in outer space.

A POST-TERRORIZED WORLD

If you are looking for some kind of acceptance,
        you're not going to find it.
This isn't the best news in the world;
it's not like you're dead,
        it's worse.
Can't you see you've hurt your father?
Go to your room.

But of course, it's nothing like that anymore.

We are very disappointed in the decision you have made.
We don't want you having any friends over this summer,
        or ever!
we don't know which ones have diseases
and I have to look out for my family's health.
We want you to move out of here by the end of the summer.
We have to look out for our family.

It's completely different now, of course.

Thank God you weren't named for your father.
At least that name will continue.
You'll live a lonely life,
        die young,
and none of your friends will show up to your funeral
because they'll be too busy having deviant butt sex.

It hasn't been that way in years.

All throughout history,
God has given us plagues to punish us.
We've had frogs, toads, locusts,
and now we have a plague of AIDS
        to punish us for gays.

But what about straight people with AIDS?
That's because you gave it to us,
        and like other plagues,
it hurts everyone, not just the target.

They haven't felt that way in forever.

We don't want you kissing any one.
        I understand
No, we mean we don't want you kissing us.
We don't want you to kiss us anywhere on the face
and we don't want you hugging us.
If any of my relatives ask for a kiss,
you either kiss them on the forehead
        or off to the side of the cheek.
If you give any of our relatives any diseases we will kill you.
Is this why you went to confession all those times?

It's really just silly to look back at these things.

We won't see you in Heaven.
Can I get you the Catechism?
Don't give us that homosexual liberal spin garbage to justify you!
If you use that damn Facebook
to spread your homosexual propaganda
        like 'this is who I am'
or 'I'm as queer as a three dollar bill,'
        we will kill you.
If you tell any of my relatives,
        we will kill you.

It's nothing like that at all now.

Whenever I look at you,
all I can see is you having deviant butt sex
with a man in a crack house!

It was just scary for her.

We'll always love you.
But we can't condone your choices.
It's like you were an axe murderer;
      we would still love you,
but we couldn't condone you murdering people with axes.

It just didn't make sense to him.

SETH RUGGLES HILER

SLASH

SETH RUGGLES HILER [Cover Artist] is most influenced by geography and the communities of his surroundings. He creates and records connections to people and place through painting and drawing. Seth received a BFA from Syracuse University in 2002 and an MFA from the New York Academy of Art in 2005. He is the Visual Arts Professor and Arts Program Coordinator at Bard High School Early College in Newark, New Jersey. His work is shown in solo and group exhibitions at galleries and institutions throughout the Northeast and in Toronto. Solo exhibitions have been presented at New Jersey's Monmouth Museum and Gallery One in Newark, at Manhattan's Duo Multicultural Arts Center and SAGE Center, and at Syracuse University. His art has previously appeared on the covers of *Assaracus* Issue 06 and Bryan Borland's debut collection of poems, *My Life as Adam*.

Please visit this artist's website and let him know you appreciate his contribution to Assaracus.

www.sethruggleshiler.com

SUBMIT TO *ASSARACUS*

We encourage submissions to *Assaracus* by self-identified gay male poets of any age regardless of background, education, or level of publication experience. For more information, visit us online. [siblingrivalrypress.com]

SUBSCRIBE TO *ASSARACUS*

Visit our website to subscribe to *Assaracus*. Your subscription buys you four book-length (120+ pages), perfect-bound issues of our grand stage for gay contemporary poetry. Our standard subscription prices are $50.00 for one year/United States; $80.00 for one year/international. Inspired by the long-running journal *Sinister Wisdom*, we are also proud to offer a special hardship subscription price of $20.00, which includes four issues of *Assaracus* shipped anywhere in the world. We ask that you pay full price should you have the ability to do so, but one's degree of good fortune should never impede access to poetry. Likewise, we will provide free copies of *Assaracus* to LGBTIQ support groups, mental health facilities, and correctional facilities by request. To request a free copy or subscription, please email us. We also offer the option of voluntary "sustaining subscriptions" for various dollar amounts should you wish to financially contribute to the longevity of *Assaracus*. Such support will also help us to continue offering discounted and free issues of the journal to those who might benefit. [siblingrivalrypress.com]

NEW & NOTEWORTHY

Prime: Poetry & Conversation by Darrel Alejandro Holnes, Saeed Jones, Rickey Laurentiis, Phillip B. Williams, and L. Lamar Wilson. Poems by and dialogue between five of the most exciting young, black, and gay poets writing today with a special introduction from Jericho Brown. (SRP)

All Men Are Afraid by Bill Trüb. Through chance encounters and sideways perspectives, in which the space between words bristles with questions of identity, Trüb immerses the reader in worlds that are as uncertain and mutable as they are poignant. (Cinnamon Press)

absentMINDR

POEMS BY TOMMY PICO WITH ART BY CAT GLENNON

for iOS mobile & tablet devices
Developed by VERBALVISUAL

Playful,
exy, anxious
nd poignant" -Leigh Stein

Beautiful, beautiful, beautiful"
-Alexander Chee

Available on the
App Store

CPSIA information can be obtained at www.ICGtesting.com
Printed in the USA
LVOW06s2047300614

392397LV00002B/7/P